PLAYING

BY THE RULES

DOES NOT

WORK

Adam and Denise

Love

Louise

X

LOUISE THOMAS

PLAYING

BY THE RULES

DOES NOT

WORK

The first 49 years

Matador
9 Priory Business Park,
Wistow Road, Kibworth Beauchamp,
Leicestershire. LE8 0RX
Tel: (+44) 116 279 2299
Fax: (+44) 116 279 2277
Email: books@troubador.co.uk
Web: www.troubador.co.uk/matador

ISBN 978 1784621 810

British Library Cataloguing in Publication Data.
A catalogue record for this book is available from the British Library.

Typeset in 11pt Adobe Garamond Pro by Troubador Publishing Ltd, Leicester, UK

Matador is an imprint of Troubador Publishing Ltd

For Henry

Prologue

The journey my soul is taking often makes no sense but when you look at the whole picture, maybe it does.... I need to keep focused and learn by my mistakes.

Is our whole life preordained? How much free will do we have and control over situations which happen to us? Can we change course if the current route isn't suiting us? Maybe it is all meant to be and we make the best job of it as we go along in order to grow.

Chapter 1

I t was so stiflingly hot, wrapped up tightly in the blankets like swaddling clothes, in the heat of the linen cupboard for the first three days of my life. My cheeks were burning red. Separated from my mother, and pushed away from the other newborn babies in the nursery for crying so much, I now became silent, bewildered and frightened. As my birth had been so traumatic, there had been fears for my survival, and the Priest had been called to give me the last rites. Thankfully he was not needed.

The feelings of rejection continued for many years, compounded by a marriage to a man without the emotional and physical needs I myself had.

During my childhood I was aware that my father adored me. However, although the day to day care was excellent from my mother, she was rather cold towards me. She would often say, "you're not one of us" and "I don't know where our Julie comes from, she is too posh for this family." She also chided me saying how silly I was as a child informing her that I often started sentences with, "when I was big and you were small…"

The jealousy she felt for her eldest child did not leave her and remained until the day she died. This was borne out of her own pain at never knowing who her own father was and seeing her daughter have something so precious she never had.

The journey we make as souls, learning, teaching, inspiring others can be full of pain. The bigger picture for me is that we have all lived before and we shall live again. Love is the only answer. We can all learn to love more.

Chapter 2

As I sit here on my balcony, and it has always been a dream of mine to have my own balcony, looking out towards the sea, just in view of the Mewstone where the river Dart meets the sea, I feel an inner contentment and calm in my soul that I have never before known. The sea captivates and enthralls me when it is calm and equally when it is rough in stormy weather. To just stare out to the horizon and think and dream and take in deep breaths is purely magical and therapeutic. Living here, I see this view daily and a whole host of the most glorious and dramatic English coastline views there are. It is simply breathtaking in parts and a privilege to know. Nothing beats the air from the sea especially in winter time apart from maybe the alpine air I had experienced skiing.

Finally I lived where I wanted so my soul could enjoy a rest except that my personal life was anything but calm. This last year ranks in the top three worst years of my life. It has literally been hell on earth and I say that from someone who has been through the most horrific pain. Living with a mentally ill person refusing to take their prescribed medication, is like living each day agonising about what time the bomb will go off. It is quite terrifying. The unpredictability of the situation is horrendous. It is not a melodramatic joke to say that I would be lucky to get out of this alive.

After years of terrible grief, pain and anguish I had decamped from my home in the Midlands to the South Coast for a much needed rest. I had never had any time alone to grieve for my son, having two other children and a husband to look after when he died in an accident, and then another two children in quick succession, after his death.

I am sure I would not have taken the bold step to move 200 miles away on my own from where I had always lived had it not been for a truly acrimonious divorce which rumbled on for years. But because of that and the actions of the children, whilst I had always been beholden to everyone in the past, now I was free to do as I pleased for the first time ever. No one was telling me off for being me and I had only myself to answer to. For the first time in my life I could just look after me and when I first arrived, the peace I felt was indescribable.

On reflection, and hindsight is a wonderful tool for which to punish ourselves, being more vulnerable than I realised, I had married for the second time in haste and we all know what to say to that, "marry in haste, repent at leisure." However, I did not know that I had married someone with serious mental health issues who often became violent and aggressive especially when not taking his prescribed medication. Ending up in hospital with a battered unrecognizable face was the end of the marriage for me after only eight months but I am trapped here in my dream location with the house up for sale. The threats I receive on a daily basis will not make me leave until I can do so with my money from the house and in the midst of all of this anguish, I have the sea. I reasoned that I only had myself to blame for spoiling the calm situation I had created living on my own.

Anyhow, as an old friend of mine used to say, "Onwards and upwards!" and "we are where we are, so let's just get on with it."

More of this later. I believe that how we deal with tragedy and pain and hurt is the answer to coping. Not denigrating how difficult that is or to be scornful of someone who struggles to cope, as I know all of those feelings. However, through stoicism and tenacity and a will to survive you can live with tragedy albeit not happy in a way you would like or choose but you have to find the best life for yourself you can. Only you and you alone can do this. If you find a partner who loves you and you love them and you are on the same path at the right time together, then all the better, but far preferable to live alone content than in sadness being with another person for the sake of it.

After deciding to not go to university following my 'A' levels, because I was in love with Peter my future husband and couldn't bear the thought of being away from him for three years, I was very happy with this new life we were planning and we became engaged. Our engagement dinner for the two of us was at The Martinez Hotel, Cannes. I was so happy that day and kept looking at my topaz and diamond engagement ring. The dinner was amazing sitting outside and I was excited that we were going to have a wonderful life. We stayed at his parent's beautiful house in Les Hauts de St Paul.

The first month of marriage was so exciting. Playing house and organizing the cooking, shopping for the ingredients on the way home from work. I thought that now I was setting the rules for future happiness. I truly believed behaving correctly would give me the contentment in life I was searching for. I had no idea how young and naive I was and now when I look at my own children, I am filled with horror that they may contemplate a move at such a tender age.

Two weeks after returning from the skiing honeymoon, I realized that my period hadn't arrived. In those days home pregnancy testing kits were rather basic so I visited a pregnancy advisory unit in Birmingham where they did the testing for you. I was shocked when confirmed with the news that I was pregnant and was immediately given a date of 3rd December for the due date of the baby. Bless her, Hannah did not disappoint and arrived on the day at 8.35 am in the morning. I was so proud of becoming a mother to a little girl. Although Peter had typically followed the male line of declaring of course my first born will be a son, he was stunned and delighted that Hannah was a girl.

Peter was more surprised than I expected him to be about the pregnancy, but very pleased. However, he made it clear that sex was now off the agenda completely. I didn't realize that the daily sex we enjoyed during the two week honeymoon was to be the only regular sex of our twenty year relationship. I said to him, "you have got to be joking, sex is normal during pregnancy," but he replied emphatically, "no, it might hurt the baby, we must not do it." I had no idea that I had signed up to a virtually celibate marriage, but I was soon to realize that sex in Peter's eyes was for making babies.

As I sat digesting this, a panic rose in me, a feeling of foreboding that I was completely dealing with an unknown entity. I was yet to realize fully that whilst for me, sex was an essential and vital part of a relationship between a man and woman, he did not feel the same.

Peter had what he wanted, a wife and a baby on the way. I felt wronged, twenty-one years of age, married and up the duff after hardly any sex. I should have been grateful there and then as there was worse to come.

The love affair I had planned in my mind for us was doomed from the start. It never had a beginning because we were poles apart and whilst I embraced my needs for physical love, Peter pushed his away for ever. The dominant control freak he was to become, had its roots in the abuse he had buried deep into his soul.

I felt strangely resigned to my situation and really hoped that it would improve. The naivety of the young lies in eternal optimism! I remained married for seventeen years having four more children and suffering the greatest tragedy of all. There is no greater pain for a mother to see her own child dead. How a strong and healthy boy can die so quickly and needlessly is still impossible for me to reconcile. I can still hear his laughter in my head even though it is twenty years since he died and I cry for him every day.

"Are you fucking listening to me you stupid bitch?" I ducked as the book he had thrown went flying past my head. "I said don't call Derwent without checking with me first. Do you understand?" Debbie the new girl in the office who thought Pete was the best boss since sliced bread, was visibly shocked. I had used my own initiative to call a customer but Peter wasn't happy. The writing was already on the wall and we weren't even married at this point, just two years into our relationship. I decided to ignore this outburst. At my peril. The signs were all there. At this point I made excuses for his behaviour, simply because I loved him.

The two years of working together running our own business, before our wedding had obvious ups and downs. It was very exciting indeed working for ourselves. The early days were tough. I had a job working as a word processor operator for an insurance broker, whilst Peter made the sales calls during the day. He collected me each day at 5 pm to go back to the office and then we would spend the evenings with me typing up the invoices and quotations on an old golf ball type writer which was laborious to say the least. It was so cold in this large office we had rented that often Peter would have to hold my fingers to warm them up for me to carry on typing. The building had been used as a temporary morgue during the war. No wonder. It was freezing in there! This was love I thought, working towards a lifetime together.

The business started to make good sales and after six months of this arrangement, I gave up my job at the insurance broker and we started working full time together, moving to larger offices to accommodate more staff. We actually worked quite well together. Peter is a natural salesman, full of the charm and cheeky blarney required in those days to get through to the relevant person. I lost count of the times I questioned him on his flirting with receptionists to do this. Another sign I ignored.

My organizational skills, combined with this, provided an excellent business model. He was unforgiving on sales targets and I was unforgiving on the accuracy of the paperwork and the systems in place for the correct dispatch of the goods. I also ran the credit control with military precision.

We became great friends with Steve, our accountant who patiently showed me how to complete VAT returns and PAYE. I am always grateful for the confidence Steve gave me at the age of nineteen and I thought I was very important completing these tasks in the business. I really loved my job.

Everything was really looking good. Or so I convinced myself. It astounds me how the heart can hide what it feels and we pretend we are content probably through fear of the unknown. What we know feels safe. There is no mystery. However, I only had to go back and look at the previous two years and what happened on our wedding day. It was all there. Plain as day.

FEBRUARY 1986

"I have been searching for inspiration on the groom's speech and was even at it in Dillons book shop this morning!" Raucous laughter emanated from the assembled guests at the wedding breakfast, of the unintended innuendo. Peter carried on holding court enjoying giving his speech, whilst I sat there in my white Italian silk wedding dress wondering if he would ever do that thing that most grooms do of saying how lucky they are to have this beautiful woman to be their wife, and how gorgeous she looks as a bride. I waited in vain. Now, twenty eight years later, when I stumbled upon a small snap a friend of mine had taken at the time, I have to catch my breath seeing how young and pretty I was.

Due to the delay of the photographer and the journey in the horse and carriage to the church, I had arrived very fashionably twenty minutes late. I was rather proud of this at the time.

So, at the end of Peter's speech, he seemed to remember that he had just acquired a wife and as a footnote, added, "thanks Ju for turning up finally!" More raucous laughter emanating from the guests. Everyone was having such a great time. It was left to my father to say how beautiful I looked on my wedding day. Nice touch Pete.

I have never been to a wedding either before or since my own where the groom has never spoken of his new wife in glowing terms. My heart was pierced that day.

Chapter 3

Hannah's birth was a truly joyful occasion. I could not believe that I had grown this amazing little girl inside of me, she was so perfect and so pretty. The pain of labour was horrific and I thought I was dying and would never be able to push her out, but the moment she was, I was over whelmed with love for her. The pain was quickly forgotten and I set to bonding with my precious little girl. Peter had spent most of his time during the last stages of labour with his brief case on the end of the bed trying to sell computer supplies to the consultant who was there for the birth. I took a large dose of gas and air to null the pain and spoke unintelligently. Peter said sarcastically, " I think she's had enough of that." There really is a reason why men cannot give birth. They could not cope.

Although clearly delighted to have a daughter, Peter soon announced that he was really tired as he had missed out on a night's sleep and needed to go home to rest. Bless him.

I started breast feeding Hannah which I found extremely difficult to do at first but had the help of a wonderful health visitor, Margaret, who told me steadfastly that I had to make a choice of letting this little baby be in charge of me or me of her.

I was very proud of myself for persevering with the breast feeding. However, when I stopped and they inevitably shrank from the large swollen milk breasts, Peter took a look at my breasts one day and said, "Oh my god what has happened to them? They are really small now." He might as well have slapped me across the face such was the sting. "They look like two flat pancakes."

Miraculously, Peter's interest in me sexually reappeared now that this little baby was in our lives.

I was puzzled by this, but as usual I reasoned that maybe everything would be as I had hoped now and we could get back on track. He kept reminding me how young he was (despite him being two years older than me) and everything had been a big upheaval for him and he was stressed.

He pestered me for a couple of weeks to have sex again before I agreed. My consultant had said don't feel under any pressure for at least six weeks after the birth and only when you think you are ready. I wasn't ready.

The first attempt was very clumsy and I did not feel comfortable or like joining in at all. A couple of weeks later we tried again and I was pregnant with our second child. Jack was born just over a year after Hannah. He was an amazingly calm baby unlike his big sister who was difficult to settle in the evenings.

The birth was truly dreadful with Jack as he lay posterior and gave me a lot of trouble giving birth to him, but as soon as he was born, he was simply serene.

Naturally, the same 'no sex' rules had applied during the pregnancy and I really wondered what on earth I had done. I became incredibly lonely at home with these little two but I revelled in watching these little people grow. Hannah was a real fuss pot around her little brother at first mistaking him for a doll. She is very intelligent and from a young age it was possible to talk to her even when she couldn't talk, so she soon understood she had to be very gentle with him.

I wondered if it were possible to hug and kiss these children too much. I hoped I could give them everything, not just in terms of the material things in life, but that I would always be there for them. I would die for them.

Jack's illness at the age of five weeks put me in a state of panic and sheer fear that I never believed was possible to feel. He started to be uncomfortable feeding. I had been breast feeding him and when he was a month old decided to give him a bottle in the evening out of sheer exhaustion. Two babies in 13 months had taken their toll on me. He almost immediately started projectile vomiting which at first I thought was the milk. I took him to the GP the following morning who misdiagnosed him with a tummy upset and prescribed him with dioralyte for dehydration.

The following day Jack was worse and I took him straight back to the doctor. "I am really worried about him, he has changed so much from a contented baby in two days," tears streaming down my face. The GP examined his abdomen and could feel a swelling. "I'll call an ambulance, he said you must take him straight to East Birmingham Hospital." "Why can't I take him to Solihull Hospital, it's only down the road." "He may need an operation so you must take him there." I called Peter and told him to meet me there.

I was so frightened and poor Jack was so hungry. He was screaming his head off, his little five week old face contorted with pain. The doctors were very quick to examine him and diagnosed pyloric stenosis. The muscle from the stomach to the intestine closes. It is common in baby boys of this age. They said it is heredity and there will be a close family member with it. It transpired that my uncle, my father's brother had had the same condition and was one of the first to have the operation forty years before.

The operation was scheduled for the following morning but between now and then Jack could not be fed. This was excruciatingly painful for both of us. There was no sleep that night for us. He was literally starving and my breasts were full with milk. How we got through that night, I do not know. There were lots of babies on that ward crying, most of them alone. I prayed to the Lord to see us through. My baby was at least being held by his mother, the other little mites were all alone.

Walking down the long corridor to the operating theatre with Jack in my arms, I thought I would pass out. A lovely male nurse called Simon walked beside me, whilst Peter trailed behind like a lost soul. When I handed Jack over at the theatre I pleaded with them to please be careful with him.

When they brought Jack round, he was not a happy boy. His little cry was croaky and he needed feeding. The doctors would not let me feed him as he had to be monitored with very small amounts of milk to check that his system could cope and that the operation had been a success. I wish I had been more insistent and fed him myself as that was the best thing for him. I was to become a prolific breast feeder in the coming years and no one would have dared question me in the future. However, here I was all alone. My mother and mother in law were of the bottle feeding generation and they simply didn't understand. I had no support system there.

I stayed in the hospital with Jack for a week. Hannah stayed with Peter's mother and father. I didn't think it was possible to feel more wretched. I was hardly eating as I felt sick with shock. The visits to the not very pleasant East Birmingham hospital toilets were all about trying to manually express my milk as my breasts were now so engorged that red patches had appeared and they were so painful I could hardly move my arms.

When we took Jack home, he thankfully settled very quickly and started to take to his bottle. I continued to breast feed him half of the time to let the milk gradually go and to comfort him. Within a couple of weeks, you never would have known the distress this little chap had felt. He recovered so quickly, my relief was palpable. Everything now was going to be ok.

Chapter 4

I had a lot of fun with these little two but longed to be back at work. From starting a business a such a young age to now being house bound with a baby and a toddler was a culture shock. I had already broached the subject of employing a nanny when Hannah had been a baby and was stunned at Peter's reaction. I interviewed a couple of professional nannies with excellent references but he found fault with both of them rather unjustly. For a young man, his ideas of the husband and wife role were decidedly old fashioned. I hoped all would improve.

They say youth is wasted on the young and I was certainly extremely naive to keep hoping that we would see eye to eye. I am no shrinking violet but the less than subtle manner in which Peter's controlling behaviour was infiltrating major decisions in our life started to affect the way I behaved. Gradually everything was turning out just as he wanted it. I was becoming a distant reminder of the vibrant young girl I had been.

Hannah first started attending a nursery part time when she was nearly two years of age and Jack followed suit. I had found myself in a position to go back to work whilst they were at the nursery and for the first time since I had married, I felt contented. To be a person again and not just a wife and mummy was essential for my well being. I had it all now, I really did. Well, almost. If we could just work on the emotional intimacy.

I could go back to being just Julie for a few hours a day. To have space in my thoughts, whilst I was driving to the office. It was pure bliss to go to the toilet without children accompanying you. To drink a cup of coffee and enjoy it in peace, was just a simple pleasure but one which can be impossible with little ones.

I was now back on the pay roll so there was freedom to buy myself something without paying from the joint account and having to explain myself. The parameters of money need to stringent if you are planning to spend the rest of your life with someone. We had none in place except for the naivety of sharing everything. I had, at this point, no idea of the power and control Peter was wishing to exert over me. I would have run as fast as I could out of St Augustine's Catholic Church on 22nd February, 1986 if part of the vows had revealed that. From day one of our marriage I saw that we were equal partners in this. We both enjoyed running the business and having children was very important too. It was all going to be plain sailing from here.

"How much did that suit cost?" Peter enquired accusingly. "Sorry? What are you on about?" I replied. "I said, how much? We don't have money to throw away you know. It's too expensive in that Madeleine Ann." I stared at him. I knew I looked good. Two pregnancies in quick succession had left me with a stone in extra weight but I had lost this and a bit more and I felt confident for the first time since the births and Jack's operation. I had often caught him staring at me in the office when I was talking to members of staff. It was plain to see in his eyes that me being a person away from the roles of wife and mother, angered him.

The business was starting to grow. A large sales team was established and we were soon out growing the premises. Peter's father, had been interested in becoming involved for some time. I had my reservations as he was continually borrowing money from the business and never paying it back which to this day, God rest his soul, he never did. I have some wonderful treasured memories of being with him on my own shortly before he died where confidences were shared and relations healed.

We started looking at premises to buy and expanding the business. It was a very exciting time and although I felt that I was getting the least sex in the world, I still felt positive about the future. I was proud of this little family and the business that we had created together. If only the passion had been there. Because, despite all my concerns, I loved Peter.

I had tried many times to have the discussion with Peter about the lack of sex in our marriage but he would not countenance such a discussion. His admission to me during my second pregnancy that as a child he and his friends had been sexually abused by a male close to them, was his reason for his failings in that department. I tried to talk with him and say we could get help and work through this. I begged him to visit the doctor but he then denied that he had told me everything about the abuse. He seemed to forget that he had told me in great detail what this evil creature had made him and the other boys do. Peter claimed it had been a neighbour, but I have my suspicions. Peter's anger talking about his childhood Catholic school and his anger at me in later years for finding solace in the church, told a different story.

Chapter 5

When Hannah and Jack were three and four, we decided to go on a skiing holiday. I was very excited as this was our first skiing holiday since our honeymoon and my parents were coming with us and Peter's brother Nick and his wife Geraldine.

We had not had sex for months before the holiday and I was so used to not thinking about contraception, I certainly didn't expect any extra curricular activities on the holiday. However, most oddly, Peter insisted on sex which was most unlike him as it was always initiated by me and usually rejected by him.

When we returned home from the holiday, and I realized my period was late, (for me late is about five minutes with my twenty-five day cycle), I felt that it was impossible for one woman to be pregnant again after so little sex. It was hardly fair. I started doing calculations of how little sex I had had to the ratio of three pregnancies and looking around at other people imagining how much sex they were having.

I felt excited again to know that there was another little life growing inside me. There is nothing like seeing a positive pregnancy test and an amazing feeling of wonder.

Henry's birth was greeted with great joy. As I had experienced with Hannah and Jack, staring into a newborns' eyes, you see the depth of a soul there that defies this brand new little newborn body. The intensity of it all is simply fascinating.

I was proud to have another little boy. Hannah and Jack, at five and nearly four were excited at their new brother. Peter seemed pleased and he had me back where he wanted me again at home trapped. I was rather over whelmed wondering how long it would take this time to get 'me' back.

Thinking back now to how I felt at this time makes me feel guilty. The Vicar to whom I have great respect has always chided me on this, saying, "there is no room for guilt Julie. Guilt achieves nothing."

However, these were just normal feelings for a young woman of twenty-six years of age with three young children. My mind body and soul were tired and although I had the physical energy of a young woman, I felt much older than I was.

I breast fed Henry for three months and was pretty exhausted as he had been nine pounds born, so I was completely drained. As soon as I stopped breast feeding him, I started to regain my energy. As before, I needed to get back to work. I avoided the mums and toddlers groups as spending the rest of my life as a stay at home mum was not my style. So, as I had with Hannah, before Jack was born, I went back to work, taking Henry with me, along with all the modern day paraphernalia required to keep him content and amused in the office with me.

In the early nineties, the housing crash meant that a lot of people were in negative equity in their properties. We were lucky that we had bought our current property before this had happened. In the computer business, for us, the manufacturers all started tightening their belts reducing credit limits and cutting payment limits from 60-90 days to 30 virtually overnight.

At this point in time, Peter's father owed us a huge amount of money for which he had been paying off his urgent debts. There was no way he could pay it back and this was a constant source of rows between Peter and I. Our suppliers were chasing us constantly for payments and we were therefore on hold for further deliveries of stock.

The inevitable happened and the company went into liquidation. There followed an almost mental breakdown by Peter. He refused to speak to suppliers who were constantly on the phone. I tried to reassure him that we had built up one business together and we could do the same again. I think his male ego refused to accept the facts of the company failure but once he started planning a new company, his joie de vivre returned.

1 9 9 3

It was obvious that Peter resented the fact that I was at work with Henry. He attended nursery in the old fire station in the jewellery quarter for two days a week and the rest of the time was in an office with me.

This was imperative for me to be working as we now had to form a new company as there was no way we could salvage the original business. I started to feel more of Peter's controlling nature and disgust of me. The sarcasm which I always been on the receiving end of in my youth, now had much more sinister overtones to it. Not only did he always delight in running me down and being critical of me in front of friends, he started doing it more in the office too. "Do not defy me," became his favourite command when I voiced my opinion.

It was difficult establishing the new business as the original had gone into liquidation for more than £600,000. Peter and Chris were banned as directors for four years and me for two.

Brendan, the lawyer got Peter 'leave to act' as director for the new company, but at a cost of over £30,000. A 'phoenix out of the ashes' company was created.

Slowly things were coming together and customers remained and some of the suppliers were prepared to deal with us. Peter's father ridiculously suggested to me, one Sunday when we were having a crisis meeting about the business, that it really was no place for me with a baby and I should be at home. He promptly rushed off to a golf lunch. Steve, the accountant had travelled from Manchester as a favour to help us sort things out. He raised his eyes and said nothing.

A year after the new business had started we seemed to be back on track financially and had managed to hold on to the house and keep the children in their private schools. I resigned myself that at this time with three youngsters and only twenty eight years of age, I had made my bed and needed to carry on lying in it.

A year after the new company was started, my friend Louise suggested a night away for the two of us. We excitedly talked about a night in London to see a show, stay over and go shopping. Louise had also married young and her husband Kim kept her on a tight leash. He reassuringly informed her and later me, that I would be the only person that he would 'let' Louise go away with as he trusted me and thought me sensible. Louise is four years older than me!

I had no idea what the reaction from Peter would be to this plan so I braced myself. Peter was very fond of Louise and in his warped way I suppose he mirrored Kim's thoughts that he trusted me with Louise. Through gritted teeth he looked at me for several seconds and then said "yes, that will be a nice little break for you." Break?! One night away, after three children and five years of marriage? I shrugged my shoulders and thought, he's having a laugh with me. I imagine that he didn't count all his business trips as jollies around Europe and to Las Vegas. Of course they were all business trips, so no fun to be had on those. No fun at all.

Anyhow, I could hardly wipe the grin from my face. I was so looking forward to this BREAK!

How amazing it was to be away from the domesticity of home and to blank it all out for a short time. I realised how much I missed being just a person. I was rather astonished at the amount of male attention I received in looks and winks. I hardly ever went anywhere other than home or school and I had forgotten that I was attractive to men. I was used to criticism and I felt flattered. I do not think that the lack of attention from Peter has ever left me and I have been on dates in recent years with totally unsuitable men, just because they have paid attention to me.

Louise and I were both so excited. We first went to Covent Garden to see Louise's brother Richard where he was working and where we had arranged to park the car. Richard looked at us both and chuckled at our excitement to be free for a day. "Two grown women acting like teenagers," he said!

"Miss Saigon" is truly an amazing show. I have seen it another three times over the years and my thoughts always return to the first time. Louise and I sobbed our hearts out at the end. It was so sad but although I wasn't entirely happy, I didn't know sadness as portrayed here. I was lucky.

Richard joined us for dinner afterwards and we sat at a table next to Kenneth Branagh and Emma Thompson and other 'luvvies' of the day. Louise wanted their autographs. We had a really fabulous time.

The rest of the evening was spent in Friday's with some of Richard's friends. Later, Louise told me that she had never seen me laugh and sparkle so much as I did that night. She said I looked positively radiant. We returned to our hotel still giggling. We both woke when we felt ready to and enjoyed a leisurely breakfast.

I was content to return home, but I had no idea of the storm brewing. Driving back from London, Louise said, "we must do that again Ju, it's been amazing." I agreed. I felt exhilarated. After taking Louise back home, I was alone with my thoughts now of the children and wondering how Peter had coped. Although I wanted the see the children, I hoped that they would be in bed when I arrived home.

As I walked in through the kitchen door, Peter was lying on the sofa and he did not get up. "Hello," I said. "Get away from me, you slut," he snarled. "I beg your pardon," I stuttered. "You fucking slag, you were supposed to be here at tea time and it's now nearly 8pm! Where the fuck have you been?"

"I called you to say that we had met Louise's aunt and uncle and would be slightly late! Why are you talking to me like this, I've been with Louise's family!" Peter's eyes stared at me with such contempt. "If you think I believe that, you're fucking stupid. Now piss off." "I cannot believe you're talking to me like this, I've been away for one night!." "As far as I'm concerned, you've been gone for two nights, so see how you feel about this!" He marched into the laundry and grabbed a holdall.

I went upstairs to check on the children. They were all sound asleep. I heard Peter banging doors and opening drawers in our bedroom so I sat on the bedroom floor in Hannah's room and waited. The next thing I heard was the kitchen door slammed, and tyres screeching off the drive. Although Peter had stormed off before, I just accepted he needed to let off steam sometimes. This was different though and was to become the pattern of his behaviour for the next ten years.

Reasoning with Peter always became a lost cause. The reassurance I received from Mr McCormick, a psychologist some years later comforted me that I could do no more. I saw the marriage as a partnership but he simply thought he was in charge and I was simply there to do his bidding. His behaviour mirrored that of a Muslim husband, not that of a middle class white English businessman, said Mr McCormick. The 'Metro bar years' started with gusto now. Peter started hanging out with his new lawyer friends.

The following morning was lovely with the children, hugging and kissing me. I got them ready for school and said that Daddy had gone to work early. As soon as I got home, I telephoned Louise. "You won't believe what happened to me last night Lou." "What's the matter? Is everything ok with the children?" she worriedly asked.

I recounted what had happened and Louise could scarcely take in what I was telling her. "Ju, I have to say I didn't really believe that Peter was more possessive than Kim, but I've changed my mind. What are you going to do? Do you have any idea where he is?" "I haven't got a clue now but I can't stay in this marriage, I just can't." "What are you doing now," Louise asked. "Just going to go shopping with Henry." "Well come over to me and we'll take Henry and Polly to the park so we can chat." I said I was on my way.

Henry and Polly with just four months apart, were having fun on the little roundabout and it was terrible to watch the naivety of children whilst feeling that my world was falling apart. I hoped they would have happy, uncomplicated lives.

"Ju, have you considered what it will be like on your own with three young children? No other man will be interested in you, you know?" "I don't care," I said defiantly, "I would rather live alone than with a man who takes every opportunity to criticise me and treat me with such contempt. I am a vehicle for everyone else's needs and nothing else. I feel so stifled and I'm not even getting any sex! Do I live all my life without that just because he doesn't want it?" "Ju I just want to really think about this. No, you shouldn't live without sex, it doesn't really bother me, but you jumped in and married your first boyfriend, so this was always going to happen to you at some point." "Lou, I have tried to get him to love me, to hold my hand, to spend time together. He doesn't want to know, and now behaving like he did last night just because we were back three hours later than originally planned, I can't cope any more, I really can't." "Well I do know a friend who has just considered a divorce solicitor who's apparently very good but very expensive," ventured Louise. "Get me the number please Lou, I have to do something."

The visit to the solicitor was futile. Her advice to me centered on trying again for the sake of the children and suing my father in law for the loss of the business due to all the loans he hadn't repaid. I had absolutely no idea at the time that divorce solicitors put a price on your head and then work from there. At this point in time, there was not enough money in the pot for her, but with the anger and revenge Peter decided to inflict on me in years to come, she did very well indeed out of this break up. The time for the break up was then. And then alone. By delaying these measures increases the heartache and torture for all involved to a further point in time but with that for us, brought new life.

When you play by the rules yourself, you expect the same standards from others. I was unaware of circling gold diggers in my midst.

As soon as Peter realized how serious I was about breaking up due to this visit to the solicitor, he was angry and hurt. This time he zoomed off in his car for two days though. I have no idea where he went. Sulking and running away was alien to me. I had been brought up by parents who would shout and scream at each other to resolve their differences. When Peter returned home, the atmosphere was cool between us. The children, at six, five and nearly two were too young to notice anything amiss although Peter and I hardly spoke to each other during this time. He explained that I had shocked him by going to a solicitor and that we had too much together as a family to lose. I decided to think things through, but felt even more trapped now than ever.

Two months later, a school parents' evening for our eldest son was on the agenda and we decided to go together. I organized a babysitter who was also working for us in the business. When plans change at the last minute, it can be to avert or embrace grave danger. I was extremely annoyed when the babysitter cancelled on me at the last minute but I did not have any feelings of foreboding. I had one regular babysitter who was ill at that time, and used family occasionally as they seemed to find it rather a chore, particularly Peter's parents. His mother's regular response was, "I'd love to but,...." Therefore I was bored of asking. So, I tried my own mother who I thought would be unavailable, but she said, that she and dad would come round by five o'clock.

I cooked the children's meal of fish fingers, chips and peas and prepared everything for their bedtime ritual. My parents arrived just as I was serving their food. I left the three children sitting at the table with their grandparents, all happy and laughing. The imprint on my mind for eternity.

I met Peter on the school car park and suggested that after the parent's evening, we go into town to do some Christmas shopping and grab a bite to eat. "If we must," he moaned, "but, I'm starving."

Jack's school report was very good and he was very settled on school. It hardly seemed worth going as we were in and out of there in less than fifteen minutes. Parent's evenings for eternity then have always held a dread for me and if I can avoid going it's a bonus. What if I hadn't gone.........

Peter and I went straight into Rackhams department store and bought a few presents in record speed. I started to feel anxious and looked at my watch. 7.25 pm. The children should all be in bed by now I thought. I rang home to tell my mother that we were going to eat and would be home soon. The line was engaged. She must be talking to one of her friends, I thought.

Peter said he was literally starving now and we went to eat at our favourite Indian restaurant. I pleaded with him to just order a main course. He was piling weight on and insisted on ordering so much food when we went out, I was embarrassed. "Just shut up and let me have what I want" he snarled.

The waiter suddenly appeared at the table. "There's a call for you." Peter went to the phone and the colour drained from his face. "What's wrong?!" I pleaded. "We have to go to the hospital now, there's been an accident with Henry." "What accident? What's happened?" I screamed. "I don't know but I have to go to the toilet." "No!" I shrieked "Let's get to the hospital come on!" I had no idea my efforts to get there faster were futile. Peter seemed to be walking in slow motion. "Hurry up!" I yelled at him. Peter's father had called to say that he didn't know what had happened but that my father had called him and we needed to go to the hospital without delay.

We arrived at the hospital and my heart was furiously pounding so much that I thought it might jump out of my chest. I breathlessly explained to the receptionist I was trying to find my son and she directed me to the second floor to the intensive therapy unit. I ran towards the lifts and pressed the button but everything was going in slow motion and I couldn't think straight. Lifts or stairs, I was thinking, stairs or lifts? My mind was racing, I had to get there as fast as possible. How? How could I stop the panic rising in me. I chose the stairs but my legs would not go fast enough. They were like dead weights refusing to obey me. Run, run I implored. But my legs weren't going fast enough.

Eventually I arrived at the doors of the ITU and burst through the door. "Where's my son Henry?" I asked a young very overweight nurse. "Be quiet," she demanded, "this is ITU." "Where is he, please?" "If you be quiet, I'll take you to him." I duly followed her and the sight before me was incomprehensible. I'd only left him three hours ago, eating his tea and now he was here all wired up on a hospital bed hooked up to a ventilator. I must be in a nightmare, I thought, not my big strong Henry. What had happened and were Hannah and Jack alright? It was to be some time before I found out precisely what had happened.

I sat next to his bed and stroked his hand. He looked as if he was asleep, but I knew he was dead. So I started to pray. Family and friends started to visit all with words of comfort but with horrified looks of despair on their faces over the next sixty one hours. Every time, I visited the lavatory, I went into the same cubicle. Someone had scratched on the door, 'let him live'. I thought, I hope yours did, please let my boy live. I did deals with God that I'd do anything if he could let him live. Anything at all. Please please please let him live.

Some friends asked if they could bring us anything and Peter said he needed some apples. Yes, apples. A bag of cox's orange pippins was duly brought in and he sat and munched his way through them. Crunch, crunch, crunch. For the rest of my life I could not bear sitting next to anyone eating an apple.

Henry looked so peaceful that first night in the hospital, but the constant sound of the ventilator was a reminder that he was in a very serious way. I looked out at the black black sky and wondered how we could get Henry back. I felt guilt that I hadn't stayed at home to protect my little boy. I had failed miserably. I stroked his forehead with these wires and electrodes pinned to them, willing him to open his eyes. "Please sit up and talk to Mummy? I'm here Henry, please?"

The following day, a dainty young blond nurse came on duty. She brought me some tea and gently stroked Henry's arm whilst I drank the tea. "I'm Lucy", she offered, "I'll help you as much as I can." As we sat watching Henry in the dimly lit room, I saw a light emanating from the far corner. The light was literally coming from nowhere. It gently made its' way to Henry and bathed him in a warm glow. "He's going", I said to Lucy, "the light is taking him." "I can see," she replied. "Where did that light come from?" I asked her, "I have seen this happen before," she said. "It is common in here."

After what seemed like a long time but was probably about a minute, the light faded. I knew my son's soul had departed and would not return. It was bizarrely comforting. I prayed for whoever was with him to take good care of him. Please look after my boy, my little soldier. He's still a baby.

A tall softly spoken gentleman arrived at the bed side and said, "My name's Alan, I'm the hospital Chaplain, can I sit with you?" We told him what had just happened and he too said he had experienced this before.

Alan was a wonderful calming influence in the midst of this unreal situation. "Shall we pray?" Alan offered. "Please," I whispered. Peter seemed to need this spiritual help too and we bowed our heads and prayed at our beautiful boy's side. I do not remember the prayers we said, just the silence of focusing on the need to try to help our boy wake up. I held his lovely soft fleshy little hands and stroked them. I knew he was dead but it just didn't seem possible, he looked so perfect. His face and body didn't look dead.

"Is there anything else I can do to help?" asked Alan. Instantly, I asked him, "Please can you christen him? He hasn't been christened." "Of course, I shall return at 7pm, that will give you some time to call any family or friends you would like to be here." "Thank you Alan, thank you so much." Peter stood by and said nothing but nodded in agreement.

Alan duly arrived with some purple orchids for Henry, and christened him. I do not remember the words he used or the prayers he said, only his gentle manner and the comfort the situation gave me. Henry was dead, I could see that, although he looked as if he was sleeping. Everyone was crying and I cannot write this now without crying and my mind jumping to that scene in 1993.

The hours of the next two days extended for eternity. Nothing was happening apart from looking and sitting with Henry. Endless cups of tea were drunk and we were suspended in time. I wanted to get out of the place but I needed to take Henry with me. I pleaded with the staff to let me take him home but they wouldn't let me.

On the Sunday morning, a young male nurse came in to tend to Henry as they had fitted a catheter to him. I pleaded with him to leave him alone. "Can't you see, he is dead?! Please leave him alone." "I am sorry," he offered, but I have to do this, I am not hurting him." But he's dead, I thought, why won't they just leave him alone?

Shortly afterwards, a doctor arrived to check Henry's vital signs and he said that Henry's brain stem was starting to fail. He advised we call any family and friends to be with us. A young doctor then asked if I had thought of organ donation as that would be the optimum time for the necessary removal of organs. To this day I do not regret my decision of saying no please leave him and us alone.

They took away all the paraphernalia away from Henry and I held him in my arms. He wasn't there. I was literally holding the dead weight of my son's body. He looked like him but he just wasn't there. "Hold him," I said to Peter, "I can't," he said and looked on. "I'm sorry, but I just can't."

The nurses came to lay Henry on the bed.

The walk out of the hospital into the icily cold December morning, was one I wanted to make alone. The gathered family solemnly followed me watching my every move. I wished everyone would go, I wanted to be alone. How could Henry be dead? He had been with me for virtually every waking moment. How could I have let my little boy down so badly, by letting him die?

Ever the tactless, and unemotional, Peter decided to break the silence. "You must not close the door on having more children."

How dare he. This was something I never forgave him for. This was way beyond any realms of decency. My son's body was not even cold and he was talking about having more children. I can only guess the shock made him say this.

I needed to go and see Hannah and Jack and tell them. They were with Peter's mother. As we walked into the house, Hannah and Jack were playing in the kitchen. They knew Henry was poorly but at five and just seven years of age, they did not understand the severity of the situation.

"Come here you two," I said, as I bent down and held out my arms. "Is Henry better Mum?" asked Jack. "No darling he has died." Hannah immediately began to cry but Jack just looked puzzled. I held them both tightly. "Where has he gone then Mum? Is he in heaven?" "He is at the hospital sweetheart," I explained. "But Mum, I thought that you went to heaven when you died, so why hasn't Henry gone to heaven?" "That's right darling, but the hospital has to look after Henry until the funeral and then he will go to heaven." "What's a funeral?" I gently explained and the questions kept on coming from Jack whilst Hannah quietly sobbed, her little shoulders shaking. It was difficult to not smile at Jack's innocence and we always remembered his oft repeated question of how Henry would get to heaven, "Will they send him in the post?"

I was exhausted now and had to sleep as I felt on the point of collapse. I was insistent with Peter that Hannah and Jack's routines should be maintained and that they should be at school as usual. Looking back now, I was walking around on auto pilot. I did not want to speak about how I felt as no one could possibly know. My boy was dead and I did not know how I would be able to continue living. I did not like the fact that for most of the time Peter just stood there not knowing what to say but at least he did follow my suggestions at this time and agreed that keeping the routine going was the best for the children. At least we were in agreement.

The night before Henry's funeral, Hannah had got into bed with Peter and I and as young children do, her arms and legs were everywhere and I could not sleep so I went and got into her bed, which was the other end of the landing. I felt like my body was a dead weight and the pressure in my head was too much to bear. How could he be dead? How? Why? If only I had not gone out, if only. I lay down and started to drift to sleep when I heard little footsteps on the landing. It must be Jack up now, I thought, and got up out of bed to look. There was no one there so I went into

Jack's bedroom and he was fast asleep. I went back into our bedroom and saw that Hannah was fast asleep too. All rather strange I thought and went back into Hannah's bed. The little footsteps continued running up and down the landing accompanied by the feint chimes of a spinning top from Henry's room. I got up again and looked but no one was there. Surely it wasn't Henry? I have always believed in spirits but had had no experiences with them myself. I went and lay back on the bed and again the footsteps started. This time I went back onto the landing and spoke to Henry. "I hope you're ok darling, I will always be here for you. I am glad you still want to play with your toys. Please be safe. I love you so much."

The following morning, I told Peter what I had heard and what I had said to Henry. He said he too had heard footsteps but had presumed that it was Jack and because he knew I'd got out of bed, thought I had taken Jack back to bed.

Slowly the information came out as to what had happened but the bare facts are that my mum left Henry in his push chair drinking his bottle whilst she took the other two to bed. He was strangled by the reins on the push chair. They called it vagal inhibition at the inquest as the cause of death. He only had a small red mark on the side of his neck in the hospital.

I felt very strongly that Hannah and Jack were old enough to be at Henry's funeral but Peter was adamant that they were too young. This affected Jack's understanding of death very deeply and I believe that they both should have been there. Jack's questions continued for a long time and he was very troubled. Hannah was much quieter and kept her thoughts to herself. She was very loving with me and always rushing up to me for a hug as if she really understood how I ached.

I read a book at this time about a family whose little girl had died and how they sent balloons to heaven for her from their other children. I said to Hannah and Jack that we were going shopping to send something to Henry. They were both excited and when we had purchased bags of balloons and a pump, we went into our field and started blowing up the balloons and letting them go. The children loved it and laughed as they shouted, "here comes another one Henry!" This became a family routine for all birthdays in the future and as soon as any balloon was in sight, it would be, "can we send the balloon to Henry mum?"

After the funeral, it was difficult to understand the new life I had with two children and not three. Things were not as hectic as Hannah and Jack were at school and whereas it had been a struggle before to do the shopping and housework with Henry, I had all the time in the world now. I had been working in the office two days a week at this time and found it very difficult to face people. Generally no one knew what to say and the only thing you appreciate at this time, is someone saying they are dreadfully sorry. It still astounds me how many people pass comment and make suggestions when they have not experienced losing a child themselves. I found most people's reactions to be crass, and extremely rude. All they need to say is that they are very sorry. No need for their unwanted views. Some people boldly informed me that if their child died then they would not be able to survive. What did they want me to do with two other young children? Kill myself? Some said that yes that is what they would do. That said, I received some wonderful heartwarming letters and cards from lovely friends and people I did not know very well. I really appreciated those and thank everyone who sent them.

I said to Peter at this time, that I wished I was dead. I wanted to be where Henry was and dead was where it was. It was where he was. Peter said I was mad and did not understand my responsibilities to Henry as his mother. It didn't mean I was going to kill myself. He didn't understand. He wasn't Henry's mother.

For the next year I immersed myself in books, anything with death, reincarnation, and religious tomes of all types, I devoured. Anything to give me hope that my boy was safe somewhere and I would be with him again one day. If the spirit of Henry was alive, then I could find a way of coping with that.

My bookcase is full in particular of reincarnation stories, especially those involving children who remember previous lives and the well documented previous lives of the Dalai Lama. Although now a keen practising Christian, I yearned for the Buddhist view on reincarnation which came so easily to them. We had been indoctrinated to believe that after death, eternal life was with our Lord Jesus Christ, not coming back into another body and life.

Reading these books gave me a hope that there was somehow a purpose in this short life of Henry's and that one day this time would be just a grain of sand in the whole scheme of things. As eternal souls living many lives, one life however painful, is not so significant when compared with all the others. We need to look at the bigger picture and understand our soul and what we need to learn. I devoured these books, such was my yearning for knowledge on death. Many of them I read several times just to check I hadn't missed anything.

In particular I was fascinated by the writings of Dr Brian Weiss, a practising psychiatrist, who was a previous sceptic of reincarnation. Using hypnosis to regress patients to solve problems in their lives, he discovered many patients regressing to a time before they were born, to previous lives and indeed to the resting soul state in between lives. Patients gave so much detail which was often corroborated that he wrote about their experiences with my personal favourite story being about Catherine in "Only Love Is Real."

I was fortunate to see Dr Weiss many years later at a seminar workshop in London and he is a very calm collected amazing being who talks so normally about this subject that you wonder why everyone does not see the world like this. It makes the most sense to me not just because I want it to, but because of my many experiences particularly since Henry's death. To live, have dreadful tragedy, then die does not comprehend with my line of thinking as I don't see the point. The pain of the loss of a child is tortuous and although I don't go along with the train of thought that it was meant to be, I do believe the events afterwards are a direct consequence. It was an accident, it didn't have to happen but it did. However hard I try, I still after all these years can't believe that it was inevitable because I want him here with me now. One day we shall all find out.

When I read Dr Weiss's "Many Lives, Many Masters" and "Messages from the masters", I had visions of the soul groups he described learning from their mistakes in previous lives and choosing actively to enter another life to learn these lessons better and to face a difficult life in order to advance as a soul. As Dr Weiss said recently on Facebook "we are here to learn, not suffer. Karma is an opportunity for growth...." I love his status updates and news of his workshops around the world.

Some years later on during an evening Peter and I had, when we went to dinner with his solicitor Brendan and his wife Mandy, the subject came up of coping with Henry's death.

Brendan, being a very direct northerner questioned me. I explained that my reading and spiritual experiences had helped enormously and the fact that I had to carry on especially for Hannah and Jacks' sake.

Brendan then surprised me by saying that he had previously thought of us being souls living many lives a complete load of tosh until his secretary lent him a book called "Only Love Is Real." An animated discussion followed with Brendan asking me if I thought that Peter and I had lived together before in previous lives. I said that I thought we had, but maybe as brother and sister. "Is that because the sex is crap?" laughed Brendan. I laughed too but Peter did not.

At this dreadful time, I imagined myself as a soul in one of these learning groups deciding on where to incarnate next and I imagined myself at the front with my hand in the air, saying yes I will choose a difficult life, I want to progress as a soul. Of course I have no idea if this is true but belief is a good thing and I have had enough contact with spirits of the dead through mediums and personally and my own astral travelling to believe in the eternal soul. A soul's understanding is entirely different to our earthly one.

I visited a medium called Gill who correctly told me of many current situations in my day to day life and that a guardian angel called William followed me around. I have no idea who this is and not a name of anyone I know in spirit. She told me that I had a very artistic daughter and a football loving son. She didn't mention Henry. At the end of the reading, with me so far having said nothing, she asked if there was anyone I would like to contact in spirit by giving her a name. I said Henry. She replied that she could not effectively contact with this spirit as the time wasn't right. However, she could say that this spirit had left the earth plane lying on a hospital bed with electrodes pinned to his forehead. That is when his soul departed on the Friday after the accident when we saw the light, not on the Sunday morning.

Attending church each week became a necessity for me and I found huge solace praying and in particular taking Holy

Communion. The prayers burned into me, I needed salvation and I would take it in any way that I could.

After time, I became very involved on the parochial church council and raised much needed funds for the restoration of the chapel. I really enjoyed these times. It was me taking time out from being a wife and mother and I met some wonderful friends whom I treasure.

Chapter 6

I received a telephone call from my friend Louise enquiring how I was and then launching into what I can only describe feeling as a cruel play on my emotions. Not for one moment am I suggesting that Louise was meaning to hurt me in any way. On the contrary, she had been a loyal, supportive and true friend. However, what she now told me seemed unbelievable so much so, that I did not believe it.

Louise took her time explaining to me that she had employed a cleaning lady to work in her home called Jenny. Despite the fact that daily life was going on for everyone including me, I failed to see why she was imparting this news to me considering that she knew exactly how grief stricken I was, and finding it hard to get through each day. Louise continued.

On her first day cleaning Louise's home, Jenny picked up a photograph of Henry to dust and stopped in her tracks clutching the photograph to herself. She called Louise and asked her who the little boy in the photograph was. Louise defensively asked her why she wanted to know.

"It's his mother I can feel," she explained, "this little boy is in spirit, he is no longer on the earth plane. His mother is in extreme distress and needs urgent help. I can feel her grief."

"How do you know this?" Louise asked incredulously. After

all, this was the first day she had been working in her home and she had taken her on due to the recommendation of one of the other mothers at her daughter's school. Aside from that, she didn't know anything about Jenny.

Jenny explained that her husband had died ten years previously and that she was in so much pain at losing him that she had to find where he now was. Therefore, she joined a local spiritualist church and found great solace going there and developing her own spiritual intuition.

She then pressed Louise to suggest to me, a woman she had never met, to seek urgent spiritualist help. "I cannot even begin to describe to you," she stressed, "how upset this lady is. The torment she is under is immense. She is not coping although on the outside others may think she is." Naturally a touch offended that this woman was talking to Louise about her close friend who Louise well knew was literally devastated, she enquired as to what exactly Jenny was suggesting.

"There is a visiting spiritualist at our church. She is from Seattle. Her name is Vita. When I go to the next meeting on Wednesday I shall ask her if she will speak with your friend. Vita is amazing and simply the best spiritualist I have come across in ten years. Please tell your friend of this conversation and tell her that she is welcome in our church."

Louise duly relayed this information to me and although this was exactly the sort of information I was craving, it seemed too impossible to be true.

However, the following week, Jenny presented Vita's telephone number to Louise with a message that I should call Vita and she would happy to talk with me.

Even though I was to talk to someone who could help me on my spiritual journey to deal with my tragedy, I did feel sceptical about how this was going to develop or indeed assist me in anyway. A complete stranger picks up my son's photo, knows he is dead and feels my pain. She then further says that a lady from Seattle can help me. Regardless of my doubts, I telephoned Vita.

When I started to explain to her who I was, she said, "I know who you are. Would you like to come and see me?"
I explained to Peter what had happened and he was sceptical although I cannot criticise him for this. He felt no need to read as I had been doing about death, but he was concerned that a charlatan would be looking to deceive me and swindle money out of me which was ironic really as future events would reveal.

Genuine spiritualists do not charge money. They may ask you for fuel money if they have driven to see you but when they see other souls in extreme distress they merely want to help.

I visited Vita a few days later. A lovely long blond haired peaceful calm lady opened the door to her mother's home in Leamington Spa. Vita's German mother was ill with cancer and she was here to look after her in her final days.

I shall always be so grateful that in her own difficult situation, she found time to console me with her knowledge. Although I had been told the rule about money I still felt I should ask if I could pay her for her time. "No thank you," was her firm reply but I had taken her a colourful bunch of freesias with a beautiful scent and she was very grateful and said that she would put these in her mother's room. At this time I did not know her mother was ill so later when I realised the significance, I was happy with my gift.

Vita started by saying that she only had brief details from Jenny that my little boy had died and that Jenny was concerned for me. She didn't know about the photograph in Louise's home, she had just been asked to help a tormented soul. I explained the details of why I was there through my friend Louise and Vita said that although she was happy to help me it was a shame that Jenny didn't feel that she could. She said Jenny underestimated how good she was at perception in these situations and how far she had herself developed spiritually.

Vita then asked me what had happened to Henry and how he had died. It was clear from the initial meeting that she believed I was still locked into the accident which had caused his death and that this was not a place for me to remain. The guilt was keeping me there. The guilt. It was my fault he was dead, I was his mother. He had grown inside of me, therefore it was my fault. The logic for me was simple and it was correct and just that I felt this guilt. I deserved to feel like this as I had let him down.

When I explained all of my feelings in this way, Vita almost threw up her hands in horror, then steadied herself and said that no, this was not the way forward and that I had to let go of these feelings as they would end up destroying me.

She then extended her spiritual beliefs and belief in God although not one God for this religion and one God for another, just God the creator. The souls that we all are have a colourful, a word she kept emphasizing, very colourful experience just by being. As a soul, either incarnate or not.

Of course I was desperate for knowledge of Henry, that is why I was there, and although she did not give me any direct message from him, she said that his soul left his body almost immediately after the accident and whilst I don't know this for sure, I felt comfort and I hope it is true. I didn't want my little boy suffering and in pain struggling to breathe.

Vita explained as had my doctor some time previously, that Henry's death happened just once. One time. Once. I was reliving it every minute of every day, and tormenting myself continually, habitually, and unnecessarily so. This was easy for others to say but for me, I could not stop the thoughts. My guilt was driving them.

Spiritualists like Vita are so calm when they talk of our souls' journey that it is impossible to not become absorbed whilst listening. Naturally I want to believe every word she says and although I am comfortable sitting here, I am aware that I don't have the conviction she does. For her, when she talks about our individual soul and the lessons it learns on each journey, in each life, it is as others discuss in casual ways what's going on in their everyday lives. What to eat that day, how work is, where to go on holiday, all general topics of conversation, nothing deep or meaningful. She was an amazing help to me and I believe to Henry's soul and my other two children.

I asked her who was looking after Henry in spirit and she said Aunty Vi. This name meant nothing to me so I asked around family members if anyone knew who this could be. Vita had given me a description of Aunty Vi which I kept to myself. Peter's mother told me that she had an Aunty Vi who had died some years before and had never had any children. I pressed her to describe Aunty Vi's physical features and she described her as a slightly taller than average woman with soft fluffy hair and a lovely smile and wearing a pristine white full length starched apron with frills around. This was the exact description Vita had given me.

I wanted to ask if she could see Henry and exactly where he was now but I realised that Vita was trying to help me let go and live again so I kept quiet. She sensed this unease in me and asked what I would most like to know. I said I would come back again soon if that was ok with her to talk further as my head was spinning at the moment. Vita suggested that I should think of going on a retreat to regain my energy. I said that would be impossible as I had Hannah and Jack to look after.

I was in a deep sleep, aware that I was dreaming but I could not move at all and my body was so still that I was conscious that if I tried to move, it would be impossible.

Starting simultaneously from my head and my toes I was sucked up and drawn out from the centre of my body. I went straight up through the ceiling and through the roof. This felt so free! Aware that my soul had left my body, I felt wonderful and never looked back even for a second. Willingly, I was going along with this as I experienced such peace, such calm, it was amazing to feel like this. The only peace I had felt since Henry had died, and it was all consuming. I was conscious and yet had no concern whatsoever for my body I had left behind.

It would be wrong to describe the experience as flying more like floating at a fast speed and a weightlessness which carries neither pain nor fear, just exhileration.

I had no recollection of returning to my body. However, upon waking up normally in the morning, I realised that I had had an out of body experience.

The following day when I visited Vita again, before I said anything at all, she told me I had been astral travelling and that I remembered my experience. I was astonished. "How do you know?" I asked her, "It's in your aura," she explained, "you have been with Henry, I can see you. You've been flying with him holding him in your arms. I can see his face looking at you and you are so happy."

At this point, I have burst into uncontrollable tears as I am now, writing this, almost twenty years later. Now, in order to compose myself, I have to go and look at Henry's picture, the last photograph of him I took. His smiling cheeky grin and sparkling eyes, with his beloved checked cap on, looking at me. Looking at me. I was furious with myself for not remembering that Henry was with me the night before. Absolutely furious! Such an uplifting and profound experience it had been for me, the first time I had been aware of being out of body and yet I didn't remember the most important and crucial detail.

"Why Vita, why don't I remember that I was with Henry? " "I don't know," she replied, "either you are not ready yet or too afraid, but don't worry that will come. The important thing now is realise that this happens all the time when we are asleep but we don't usually remember. Now that you do remember being out of body, you are more likely to open up to this in the future. Just be open and relax."

Now I felt I had my own concrete and irrefutable proof that our souls meet up with our loved ones again and can do so whilst one is incarnate and one is not. Many mediums countenance against trying to do this and force the issue too often, to let the souls departed be free and the living to live their intended time out on earth. For my part, I believe my grief was so intense and my yearning so great and I was of course open to the idea of truly eternal life, that my mind body and soul was not going to rest until I had my own evidence. Henry was not in the white coffin in the churchyard. He was back in his soul state, watching and maybe deciding when to reincarnate. Why this had happened to him, I don't know the answer, but the agony I felt of that little boy not growing up and the acuteness of my pain, had an absolutely tiny little healing moment at this time. His body was dead. His soul was alive. Eternally.

I then asked Vita what she could see of my eternal soul. The knowledge I was accumulating forced more questions into my mind. Vita sat back in her chair and soon started explaining what she could see. I wanted to know if she could see any of my past lives.

"You are a young girl in a pinafore style dress and you are banging a stick on a toy drum. There is a nanny or governess woman shouting at you. She is very overbearing and you do not understand her anger. She is telling you to be quiet but you are just a young child playing. Looking around your nursery, there are beautiful dolls and teddy bears, it is a child's fantasy land. Your parents are quite distant, you are their only child and that is why this woman cares for you, albeit in a remote fashion. They are clearly wealthy as you live in a very large grand house."

Vita paused for a few minutes. I sat digesting this utterly fascinated and intrigued. "Goodness me," I said, "it seems odd that although I don't have any knowledge of this, it doesn't seem strange or weird. What happens to me?"

"As you grow older, you develop a lot of stomach pains and although you are seen by many doctors, it seems there is nothing they can do for you. You look about fifteen and it seems you have cancer, you are very thin and you die. Your mother is quite grief stricken, crying and then wailing over your bed. Although cold towards you, she loved you very much. It wasn't her fault, it was the way things were in these sorts of families. The care of the children left to others. Your soul left this body very quickly and didn't stay around for your funeral. Most souls actually enjoy staying around and watching their own funeral but you had had enough of this life and departed the earth plane the moment you took your last breath."

Vita then said that I had had a brief life and died as a baby but before my soul reincarnated in this life, had been an angel following distressed children around the world. She said I was instinctively drawn to young children in poverty. I wanted to help them she said.

The way Vita talks, is as if she can literally see this playing out like a movie in front of her. I have no idea if these lives of mine happened and a sceptic would say that Vita could use this life story on anybody. Quite so. However, when you are faced with a scenario where someone unknown to you in your normal everyday life, who clearly possesses pyschic ability, talks to you in this way and you experience the power and presence of a soul rather than a human being talking, it is profoundly therapeutic. Whether you are a believer or a non believer and I clearly fall into the first category, the immense joy that I felt focusing on Henry's soul was extremely helpful in my distress.

Vita put me in touch with a lady who was a visiting spiritualist to their church from a church in Coventry. She explained that she thought Coral was very good at her perceptions, but to be mindful of the slant Coral put on things rather than just relaying what she saw.

I telephoned Coral and asked her if she would meet me but mindful of the distance from where I lived, suggested I visited her. She emphatically replied that she would visit me if I just "gave her a fiver for her fuel."

Coral got lost on the way and I had to go out in my car to find her which considering that we had no mobile phones in 1994, wasn't that easy.

I drove towards the Coventry Road to where she had last called me from a telephone box and my eye caught a black lady standing outside an austin allegro car in a side road and I instantly knew this was Coral. This was strange as I didn't know the colour of her skin prior to this, let alone the type of car she was in. As I drove over to her she immediately started waving and saying "Julie I just knew you'd find me!"

Coral followed me home and she was an animated full of life

soul who talked extremely quickly. She recounted how her daughter had died from cot death and the resulting struggles she had experienced coping, but cheerfully concluded that if her daughter had lived she could be giving her a right load of grief now. I couldn't believe my ears! She saw the horror in my face and said that I had a long way to go as far as understanding it all. Clearly.

She then admitted that she knew brief details about Henry's death which was not the way she preferred, but that she had been focusing on him since my call to her days earlier and that all she wanted to do was give comfort to me by relaying things she could not possibly have known. To prove to me that he was still alive but now in spirit. He still existed, she said.

Suddenly she said, "there's a man here, he needs to talk to you, he can see your devastation and he just wants to say hello and to tell you to have faith." "Who is he?" "I don't know his name but he was a good friend of your parents and you loved him like an uncle and he died in car crash at the age of forty two."

Goodness me that was my uncle Graham. "Is he ok?" I asked. "Yes he's fine, but very concerned about your distress. He says you have to start living again."

Then of course I asked her what she could see of Henry. "Oh a delightful soul, very happy, loves his mum and dad and sister and brother and he has a secret to tell you but you mustn't be cross." I really couldn't believe what I was hearing and did not expect that she could tell me anything about Henry that I did not already know.

"Well," she continued, "there was a time recently when Henry's dad looked after him whilst you were away for a day. Henry says that his dad decided that they do some gardening together and he really enjoyed this day. It was great fun especially as his dad sat him in the wheelbarrow and raced around the drive with him, all the time saying don't tell your mum as she will go mad thinking you will be in danger. Henry says he laughed and laughed this day and understood that you would be worried, but he just loved being in that wheelbarrow!"

By now with my emotions going into meltdown, although I could believe that Peter would race around like this with Henry in the wheelbarrow, I couldn't believe that Henry was telling me. Peter knew that I would have declared this to be dangerous, concerned that Henry would fall out.

Eventually I thanked Coral for her time and she departed by saying that she was happy if I had some comfort from her visit but that I had to let go. The spirits need to go to the spirit world she declared. It was no good them hanging around here just for our sake.

I decided to think before I interrogated Peter as I needed proof that what Coral had said was a fact. Then I would know that Henry had truly sent me a direct message.

When Peter came home that evening, he knew that I had met a medium that day but I said that I needed to talk to him first before I told him what she had said.

I asked him about the day when he had looked after Henry and they had planted daffodils together. "Well, what do you mean? You know we planted daffodils that day and we were outside most of the day. What do you want to know?"

"Just tell me if there is anything which I would be cross about. I am not cross now, but please just tell me." Peter took a deep breath and said that there was nothing really except that he had sat Henry in the wheelbarrow and raced around the drive with him and had said that he mustn't tell mummy because she would tell daddy off.

I kissed Peter on the cheek and said I needed to go and lie down. This news needed digesting before I discussed it further. A direct message from my dead son to reassure me that he still existed. He had told me a story about him and his dad which I didn't know to prove it to me. To prove to me that he, his essence, was still alive.

Soon after this, Peter decided that we all needed a holiday and rather unhelpfully purchased a caravan for us to take to Spain, which I must confess was not my idea of a holiday. He also arranged to go with some friends of ours who had a two year old daughter. Although I liked these friends very much, the idea of going on holiday without my two year old child filled me with dread. I also was in a panic about not being able to go to Henry's grave every day.

As Peter had no experience towing a caravan, there were many hitches and mistakes along the way which were quite funny at times and helped to ease the situation. Any humour helps when all you feel is deep, black pain.

I should never have agreed to this holiday as so distressed did I become that instead of driving back in the car with Peter, towing the caravan, I flew home with Hannah and Jack early.

The first night in northern Spain, we settled in a camp site full of very tall thin trees, I don't know what these trees were called but it was very cool due to the trees in very hot and humid August weather.

I was in a dreadful state of anxiety that it had now been two days since I had visited Henry's grave and felt that I had left him behind.

It was quite easy getting to sleep as we were all very tired from the long drive and ferry journey. At least Hannah and Jack enjoyed the fun of it all, but I couldn't join in.

Virtually as soon as I was asleep, I felt my soul quickly whoosh out of my body, much faster than on the previous occasion, and I felt myself travelling at speed through the trees and beyond. This felt so fantastic! Before I knew it, I was rolling around on the bed at home with Henry in my arms. We were laughing and singing and I felt so happy. The whole time I was aware that my body was back in Spain and that mine and Henry's entities were weightless and timeless. I thought of Hannah and Jack and knew they were fine and fast asleep so I didn't worry about them. This was not dreaming.

I glanced around the bedroom and noticed how messy it was with the quilt crumpled up on the floor and a pile of bed sheets for washing as if someone had stripped the bed to put fresh linen on and stopped halfway through.

In those days I put so much of my energy into running the house efficiently and Peter used to say that it was like living in a five star hotel. He often remarked that no sooner had he taken off a shirt that it was washed, dried, ironed and back in his wardrobe so really he only needed two shirts at the maximum.

June was a lady who came to the house once a week to help me clean. She also occasionally babysat for the children. I had asked June to strip all the beds whilst we were away and leave them to air and put the fresh sheets on the day before we were due home. So fastidious was I that I had asked her to fold the duvets back at the end of each bed as I hated the duvets being on the floor. This wasn't right I thought as I glanced around, but I carried on cuddling and laughing with Henry.

The next morning I spoke to Peter and said that before I told him something, I wanted him to please just listen to me and not mock me in any way even if he didn't believe what I was about to tell him. He agreed to do this and then I said that I was going to give him some details, but not all, and I would like him to telephone June.

I patiently explained about my astral travelling and he listened carefully. He was getting used to me talking of soul travel and spiritualism. I wanted him to verify that the bedroom was exactly as I saw it last night which wasn't how I had left it. I needed him to phone June so I could prove what I was saying.

Peter telephoned June and she said that she was just going up to our house to change all the beds so Peter asked her to telephone his mobile as soon as she arrived there. He had to emphasise that there was nothing to worry about, but that he needed her to do something as soon as she arrived.

When June telephoned, Peter explained that he needed her to describe exactly how our bedroom looked and not to worry if it wasn't how Julie had left it or how she leaves the beds to air. June then explained that she had been in a hurry when she had stripped the bed, so the quilt was crumpled on the floor in the left hand corner and the pink and white sheets for washing were in a pile next to it. She apologised and said that she knew that wasn't how Julie did it, but repeated that she had been in a rush.

Peter assured her that she had nothing to worry about as we just needed the information. I was listening to this conversation the whole time on loudspeaker and told June I was very grateful and would explain the story in full when we got back home.

Peter looked at me and said, "Well you were right, I'd like that to happen to me and spend some time with Henry." I later relayed the full story to Michael and Sarah, our friends, and Sarah exclaimed that she had goose bumps all over and felt a shiver down her spine. Everyone believed that this had not been a dream. I knew it hadn't been a dream.

Peter's cousin Jennifer and her husband and children visited us often as their three young children were all similar in ages to Hannah, Jack and Henry. Jennifer was distraught at Henry's death and spent many hours talking on the telephone with me about how I was feeling and she was very interested in all the books I was reading to help me cope.

One day a small parcel arrived addressed to me and when I opened it, there was a small picture frame with the following handwritten words inside from Jennifer, "Henry may seem to those who don't understand to have gone before us, but for those who do understand, he is as alive as he has ever been."

This was lovely and comforting and I still have this picture frame with these words. I telephoned Jennifer to thank her but she was worried that she may have upset me and explained that she had felt compelled to send the words as they were going around in her head. I reassured her I loved her words and was very grateful for her care and support.

The next time Jennifer, Stuart, Sophie, Thomas and Huw visited us in September 1994, Jennifer told me that her son Thomas had been talking very freely about Henry and the fact that he knew he and Henry had been friends forever. Thomas had just turned four years of age. Jennifer asked Thomas explain what he meant by forever.

"Always," he replied, "we have always been friends. And before." He then proceeded to tell her that he had been talking to God checking that Henry was ok.

Now, Jennifer said she would ask Thomas in front of me, if he remembered what he had told her last week.

"Tom, do you remember what you told me last week about you and Henry being friends forever? If you do, tell Aunty Julie."

We weren't prepared for what followed.

"Yes," started Thomas, "I have always been friends with Henry and before. But I have been so worried about when I will see him again that when I go to bed I ask God if is he ok. The last time God said I could come and see him but I said I didn't know the way so God said to hold his hand and he would show me the way, and then we walked up the steps together." "That's lovely Tom," I said with a lump in my throat, "did you see Henry?" "Yes, but it made me a bit sad because I want to see him more."

With that Thomas ran off to join the other children to play.

Jennifer and I both with tears in our eyes, hugged and Jennifer said that she believed him. "So do I," I told her.

Shortly before Henry's death I had persuaded Peter to have a vasectomy reasoning that now with three children and great prospects with the business and our life, that we could have the passionate physical relationship I desired. Ever the optimist I thought we could enjoy a sex life removing my concern of becoming pregnant every time we had sex. I still cherished that we would one day have the type of relationship I craved.

After much discussion, Peter and I agreed to try for more children. This would be the best for us both and also for Hannah and Jack, we reasoned.

Peter's vasectomy reversal was a success. The surgeon who carried out the operation had by coincidence taken out Peter's appendix in his youth. He had a good success rate in this procedure but we were warned that the chances of success were not high.

The fact that the reversal was being done only a year after the original operation stacked the odds of success higher.

After the operation we were told to wait several weeks before attempting intercourse. One morning, after I had taken Hannah and Jack to school, I was so exhausted and drained that I did something I rarely did. I went back to bed.

My emotions were everywhere with this decision to try and have more children. I had been clear with Peter that I would not be prepared to have just one more child as I didn't want this child, especially if it was a boy, to be seen by anybody as a replacement for Henry. I declared that we would have two more children fairly close in age so that they could grow up close together like Hannah and Jack who have a very special relationship with each other.

As I drifted off to sleep, I was aware I was drifting out of my body but not going anywhere, just hovering above it. My body was feeling such pain, I needed a little escape.

Aware that I couldn't move my body at all, it was weird being asleep and a tiny bit conscious.

Suddenly, I heard heavy footsteps even though the bedroom floor was carpeted, these steps sounded like they were being made on a wooden floor. The steps were nonetheless emanating from this bedroom where I lay.

This seemed like a mixture between a dream and a soul travel. I sat up in bed in the dream and a tall man dressed in a slim fitting black suit gently handed me a baby. I was ecstatic.

Eleven months after this dream, George was born. Funny, happy, gentle sensitive George.

Chapter 7

George was a very good baby but often woke at night seemingly in pain. I discovered the name of a cranial osteopath specializing in treating babies and took him for a few sessions. After these he slept soundly.

It was amazing having a baby in the house but I felt a huge amount of guilt. Henry wasn't here. I decided to never let this child out of my sight. Naturally this was totally unrealistic if George was ever going to enjoy his life, but it was so difficult and I was nervous of normal ordinary life. I saw danger in everything whereas other people did not. At times I was frantic with worry that somehow something dreadful was going to happen to one of my children again.

Hannah and Jack were simply amazing with George, they loved him so much and this was a huge boost to our family to have this carefree baby as the youngest member. Peter of course was delighted and impressed that he had fathered another child.

When George was one we had a family holiday in the old favourite which is still to this day Peter's favourite, The Martinez Hotel in Cannes.

In the foyer, they had glass cabinets displaying merchandise from the local designer boutiques and in one of them was a simply stunning display of pink baby clothes. Everything for a baby girl in the prettiest and most exquisite designs.

I immediately went outside to where Peter was in the swimming pool with Hannah, Jack and George and announced that I wanted us to try now for another baby. Peter asked me what the rush was and I explained what I had seen and I had such a strong feeling that if we tried now, the baby would be a girl and a companion for George in the way that Hannah and Jack were with each other. I also stated that so fed up was I with the interference during labour in hospital that I had previously endured, that this baby would be born at home. "Oh no," Peter said, "you're not having a baby at home. No way. Yes let's try for a baby now but no way will it be born at home."

Frederica was born nine months later. At home.

Her birth was quite comical in a way despite her not breathing immediately but a tremendous midwife, Jenny, delivered her on the bathroom floor. A second midwife due to assist had got lost so Peter spent his time running up and down the stairs on the telephone to her giving directions, whilst telling me off for having too much gas and air.

Frederica was perfect. She soon found her voice and woke up George and Jack who then woke Hannah. Being born just before midnight, we were now all up for the whole night! It was so wonderful to have another baby in the house. Peter and I were very good at making babies together.

I didn't feel such guilt as before but I don't know if this was the passing of time or the fact that Fred, as she is now called, was a girl.

Anyhow, I felt blessed to have these extra children to love and join in with the fun. All four of them are exceptionally close which I treasure.

One day I was sitting on the floor changing Fred's nappy when she was eight weeks old and George was jumping up and down on the bed. "Stop it George, get off the bed, you might hurt yourself." George carried on jumping. "George please stop it!"

The following words took my breath away and were ones I never in a million years expected to hear.

"Why mummy?" George asked me. "Because you might fall and hurt yourself!" I explained. "I hurt myself. I felled out of the pushchair and I died."

A cynic or sceptic would argue that George may have heard what had happened to the brother he never knew. But George had only just started talking, he wasn't quite two years of age and we never talked about the method of Henry's death as it was simply too painful.

Of course I felt that Henry's soul was now in George hearing these words which seems a ridiculous idea in this western world of ours, but so normally accepted in countries like India. In fact they actively look out for children's recollections of previous lives and there are many fascinating tales in the writings of Dr Ian Stevenson where families will often get in touch with and become friends with the previous family if they discover their child has enough memories for facts to be verified such as names and location. The stories are very compelling.

Whether Henry's soul sent these words to comfort me, whether his soul is in George or not, I do not know. What I can say with complete conviction is that the comfort I felt was immense.

I telephoned Peter and breathlessly told him the news. "I am busy now in a meeting. Tell me later." The line went dead. The next few years were of family life and running the business.

Chapter 8

I always knew I would divorce Peter. I so strongly wanted to in 1993 and had even started planning where me, Hannah, Jack and Henry would live. I often think if I had pursued things more fervently then, Henry would still be alive. Sudden changes to your routine or plans can alter life forever.

For me, the relationship should have been at the heart of the union and the priority with the children in the middle. The children will leave and develop their own lives but the marriage should last for life. I meant the marriage vows when I said them in church but I was young and with my head full of romantic novels, and did not appreciate how I would feel when I realised that I had merely been used as the baby making machine.

By starting divorce proceedings in 2002, nine years and two more children later, I was hugely resentful of the wasted time in being happy and peaceful but figured that at the age of thirty eight, I had plenty of time to find the happiness I craved. Quite why I thought Peter would accept this and leave me alone, I don't know. I had clearly 'cried wolf' about divorce for far too long for him to realise how desperately unhappy I was and that one day I would do it.

The purchase of a large Edwardian family home in 2001, in need of complete renovation, was to prove the straw that broke the camel's back in our marriage. We financially stretched ourselves to purchase the house and I truly believed, and still do, that this was to be a make or break outcome for Peter and I to go the full distance with the 'til death us do part' vow.

Within weeks of purchasing the house and employing a small army of labourers to strip the place out, Peter was accusing me of flirting with the builders and suggesting that sexual banter and innuendo was my reason for supervising the work. Everybody with half a brain knows that most labourers and workmen down tools the minute your back is turned. The kettle's on and the 'Sun' is out. It was certainly clear to me that several of the men working on the house had an eye for me. They were normal red blooded sexual men. It was definitely in their eyes. The reality that men found me attractive still did not ring true with Peter's threats to me, "if you leave me, no other man will want you. No blokes want a bird who's had five kids with a fat arse like yours."

Sadly for him, Peter's threats did not frighten or deter me from a fantasy in my mind, that one day I would fall in love with a man equally in love with me and that there would be lots of sex. I soon learnt that most men are dirty dogs when it comes to sex and even 'the happily married ones' will cheat given the opportunity. There are lots of women like this too of course and I was shocked to discover how widespread this all was, having been cocooned for so long. To his day, I do not understand why Peter thought it was acceptable to deny me sex. I was a normal red bloodied young woman. I needed loving and I had been loving everyone else so far.

Peter was very angry to receive a letter from my solicitor asking for a divorce. So much so that he rushed a divorce petition in on me when he realised that I was not going to change my mind, so that he could declare that he had divorced me. "Male pride, ego, they all do it!" laughed my solicitor. "He's obviously been out and the bought the male guide to divorce. I guarantee you he will be as predictable as all the other husbands when the wife wants a divorce but the husband does not." Her claims of being one step ahead sadly did not materialize and she failed spectacularly to pick up on something that was staring her in the face if only she had read all the documents. However, this was not to surface until 2009 in a very underhanded and sly manner.

For a few months, Peter had persuaded me try again with our marriage for the sake of the children. He promised certain things would change and that he would make an effort to understand how I felt. This trying involved everything continuing exactly as before. Even a make or break weekend in Milan on our own, when I tried to hold his hand, but he couldn't as he had an umbrella in his other hand, and I tried to intiate sex, turned into a disaster. I gave up.

Now that nasty letters were flying back and forth between us from the respective divorce solicitors, home life was fraught with tension.

I found the name of a pyschologist specializing in relationship counselling and suggested rather tentatively to Peter that we should go to ensure harmony at home for the children. He wasn't overly keen but agreed to go.

Mr McCormick is such a quiet gently softly spoken character when he speaks, and yet possesses a mountain of wisdom regarding human behaviour and true motives. For him, every spoken word or deed done, is a pane of glass he sees through.

The purpose for me, was to talk through our situation and form a working plan to get through the divorce and house sale to keep everything calm, particularly for the sake of the children. It was never my intention to try to work on the relationship. I had been so unhappy for so long, that I now felt utterly resigned to breaking free.

Whilst we chatted in our first session with Mr McCormick, he noted that the way we talked with each other with such easy and familiar banter, it was a shame the relationship could not be salvaged. I was far too embarrassed to bring up the subject of sex at this point, this was for later on, when I was on my own. I also knew only too well how Peter would have reacted had I have done so! With fury! I also could not adequately articulate how the years of verbal abuse had ingrained deeply into my psyche. Peter's explanations when I begged him to stop being rude to me of everything being a joke and he didn't really mean the things he said, were wearing thin.

Mr McCormick quickly acknowledged how often we both brought Henry into the conversation either talking of events before or after his death. He suggested that at that time, nine years previously, it was vital for us to seek joint help, and it was such a pity we had not. The loss of the child he noted, needed both parents to be on the same page, even if they needed to grieve in their own way.

We discussed keeping the contact with the solicitors to a minimum and above all factual. It was agreed that we could live separately in the house keeping a united front for the children. All these words tripped out so easily. The reality was another matter.

These sessions continued for eleven weeks and at one point I thought we were making progress with keeping things calm between us, until the final joint appointment.

Mr McCormick suggested to Peter that he saw what was happening between us to be a battle to win and not a divorce. "Oh yes!" exclaimed Peter. "I win at everything I do! I win in business, I win at football, and I am one of life's winners! And mark my words, I will win at this."

As I sat there, with Mr McCormick's cats swirling around my legs, and I am not a cat lover, I felt sick to the pit of my stomach. So a battle it was to be and a battle it was.

When we went outside to the car with Peter still bleating on about being the winner, I could not help sarcastically saying how amusing I had found it that Peter had walked steadfastly into Mr McCormick's trap. "Trap? What the hell are you on about?" "He's got you sussed," I said, "well and truly." Funnily enough, Peter refused to see Mr McCormick again.

Mr McCormick was invaluable in my recovery from this torrid time and I continued to visit throughout the divorce and beyond. I started to open up about issues and pain I had buried deep within me.

When Peter started residence proceedings for custody of the children, some months later, my sessions with Mr McCormick were invaluable and the solicitor's advice was largely very expensive and useless. "The solicitors are only interested in planning their next holidays with your money. You should do your own divorce." "I wouldn't know where to start," I protested. "There is plenty of help available," explained Mr McCormick, "you really should think about it. The solicitors aren't any cleverer than you." I so wish I had heeded his advice, but I was so emotional at the time, I didn't feel I could do it. My energy was taken up with looking after the children on my own. The battle became an awful lot bloodier now thanks to the solicitors. I wish I had burned the ludicrous amount of money I paid as this would have felt more satisfactory. At this time, Peter was still asking me to give it all another try and urged us to have another baby together. A sure way to keep me trapped for longer. He denied this in court.

I don't know at what point Peter found himself a girlfriend or indeed if there was one during the marriage, but when he did eventually leave the marital home, he proudly announced that he had a new girlfriend. By my estimations, he had found this new girlfriend somewhere between five seconds and five minutes from becoming single again.

He was proudly boasting that she was lovely in every way that I was not, and that he was the happiest he had been in years. Although I was angry at the way he was talking to me, although I really should have become accustomed to it by now, I actually didn't care. However, this new girlfriend with a mystery identity was immediately involved with the children which was extremely upsetting. Peter had no regard for their feelings that they should want to spend quality time with him alone and they often complained to me about this. Peter marched on regardless doing exactly what he wanted to do.

When I finally escaped Peter's clutches physically, there were hundreds of men interested in me for a variety of reasons. Sex obviously being a primary, but I also met men who wanted to settle down with me and have babies! Aaaargh, this was the farthest thing from my mind!

Now that I was legally separated from Peter and I was free to choose what I wanted in a partner, I didn't have a clue. I had no experience in men, just the man I had married. I made some disastrous choices largely based upon the men's level of interest in me regardless sometimes of whether I was attracted to them. Some relationships became sexual and some did not (thank the Lord). My brief experiences of men my own age were not positive, it seemed that Peter was not the only selfish male after his own quick invention of premature ejaculation and timetable to suit him.

I was pursued by several men considerably younger than me and was flattered and keen because after all, I had never had a young man. The first one I jumped into bed with blew my mind with passion. We had been flirting for two months and meeting up at all 'the' places that singles were frequenting at the weekends. Unfortunately, he was very emotionally insecure having not seen his mother since he was a child. This was not good news for me.

The electrical tension each time we saw each other and our fingers touched for a fraction, built up so that when we finally went all the way, it was like a scene from a movie. As he deftly twirled me around, kissing me and making gentle hand movements up my skirt with me pretending to resist his advances, this was the stuff of romantic dreams! I had never been teased and caressed like this. We just about made it to the bedroom entwined in each other's arms and landed rather suddenly on the corner of the bed where the bed frame promptly collapsed. Completely unperturbed by this, we just made our way to another bed still entwined.

When I finally succumbed to him taking my clothes off, the following three and a half hours blew my mind. I had been used to three and a half minutes (if I was lucky) and this was just unbelievable. He explored every single part of me. The kissing was every bit as passionate as the love making and continued for an hour afterwards. I was in heaven. All the time we were making love, he asked me to promise I would never hurt him. I said I would not, but he seemed unsure. Still I revelled in the passion we were having and wished it would never end.

I realized the next day that this is what I wanted and craved in a relationship and had missed out on. I had explained my situation fully to Mark of how important this was to me, having only ever slept with my husband. He caringly text me the following morning to ask if I was ok. I could not reply immediately as I was playing golf, (something I wished I had cancelled and my inner thighs were aching so much, I could hardly walk!) Mark had then sent a subsequent text worriedly asking if I had received his first text. I text him back that I was ok. He was then very keen to meet up again but it was clear he was frightened of becoming involved with me with the divorce proceedings going on. We continued to meet up with the tension surprisingly still tantalizingly high, even after the deed was done.

It was so exciting going out and being pursued with the air of sexual excitement and thrill. I suppose it can only be described as going back in time and having my youth, but at a later stage.

The buzz I felt at my emerging sexuality, was against a backdrop of an extremely acrimonious divorce fuelled by the greed of both sets of solicitors, a poor court system and Peter's refusal to arrange a private settlement ourselves. At his very best, "I'm having everything, you'll see, the house, the cars, the business, the children. I will see you in the gutter without a penny." He vehemently denied his violence and outbursts towards me during court proceedings and many of his lies were believed. Although not the majority.

One consolation was that when he was lying in court, which was mostly, he was squirming and gesticulating so much so that on two occasions, he knocked over a glass of water and then a jug.

I tried to switch off from the nasty letters arriving almost daily and the relentless onslaught onto my character. I had sole responsibility for the children and despite Peter renting a flat, he refused to have the children for overnight stays. "If you think I'm having those kids so that you can go clubbing," he said, "you can fuck off!".

Being a mother is a thankless job at the best of times, being a single mother, without the support of their father is extremely tiring. Peter had stopped the bank account and credit cards and I was literally penniless, living in a one and half million pounds country property.

Amidst the backdrop of this, I enjoyed a few with nights out. With Mary to babysit the children as she had done for the last few years, I had a release from the pressure. The routine of rising every day at 6 am to drive the four of them to Birmingham to school and drive back for work, then back again in the afternoons made me feel like a walking zombie because I was so tired. Back home the chaos of homework and tea time and doing the washing and the difficult task of getting everyone into bed was draining.

The nights out were my salvation, but I was painted as a party animal in court whilst in actual fact the one having the party lifestyle and exotic holidays was him. The nights of dancing were the most fun. My friends laughed when I asked them if they wanted to come out 'to do dancing.' I needed to dance.

I visited my friend Mary whom I had met on a Christian course in the cathedral in Birmingham. She had been through a terrific battle with her ex husband for the custody of her children.

Mary explained to me in no uncertain terms that she knew exactly how it felt to have the knives out for you. As a mother you need to be saintly and not a normal human being for the courts to not believe that the children are better off in your care than in the care of a father who indulges them and gives no discipline. She declared that the belief of the court was that if a man had applied for custody it was a foregone conclusion that the mother was mental or crazy and that the father had just cause. She herself had been described as a religious zealot and a drunk in court when she was none of these things. She got custody of her children with a further very dark tale to tell of what she believed to be her husband's driving force in this dreadful battle, but that is not for me to say here.

I had escaped from the cage I had lived in for twenty years. I was free. I did not fail in my duties to my children and had to deal with huge upset from all of them. I am sorry for the pain they have all felt and none of them have forgiven me for leaving their dad. He is a wonderful happy go lucky funny man in their eyes and can do no wrong. Unfortunately Peter encouraged the children to be disrespectful to me which is in stark contrast to how he supported me in disciplining them when we were together. His favourite line, oft repeated of "don't listen to her, she's broken up our family, and now we're not going to get the swimming pool and the tennis court we planned," was tedious. He permeated their brains and continually used them as weapons against me. I told Mr McCormick at this time that it was worse now away from Peter, than when I was with him. He explained that I had always been there to temper Peter, but that now he was out of control and he was worried about the children having false memories in the future.

"What can I do to stop this?" I asked, "and when will it end?"
"There is nothing you can do Julie," replied Mr McCormick, "it will end when they put the final nail in the lid of his coffin. As you have these children together, every opportunity that Peter has to hurt you in the future as the children marry and have their own children, you will be a target."

I felt sure that Mr McCormick was exaggerating and that one day Peter would calm down. There is no sign of that happening. For me, I would be friends with Peter for the sake of the children. I had played by the rules…

Chapter 9

With Mark obviously keen to follow me to wherever I said I was going out each week, it was clear I subconsciously wanted more. On another night out, shortly afterwards, dancing in Tigi's, I met Richard. For the next four and half years we were involved on and off but only with hindsight can I see that I was not ready for such a relationship and Richard keenly was. Despite this we quickly embarked on an extremely passionate relationship. His first words to me were, "you captivate me." I was sorted! This was how I needed to spoken to.

When we met, Richard went on a golfing trip and continually texted and called me for the whole week. The anticipation of meeting up with him was delicious and after keeping our hands of each other for a few weeks the tension was rising.

After meeting for a drink, Richard casually suggested going back to his flat. It was a very close summer evening. He was good at setting the scene and I fell for every step.

After much kissing and fondling, Richard asked if I was hot and needed a shower whilst pouring me a large glass of wine. I resisted for about ten minutes which was pretty good considering how turned on I felt. It was only much later that Richard told me he went into the shower with a gorgeous woman who was prettily made up, who came out looking like Alice Cooper such had my mascara streaked down my face. Mercifully I was unaware of this and again revelled in the passion. This was to become all consuming for me and Richard because we could barely keep our hands off each other and I could not hazard a guess at how much time we spent in bed. Basically, at every opportunity and in every place imaginable we took our passion to the limit. This way, that way, up against the wall, in the car, in the bath, outside, on the chair, on the table, on the stairs, by the fire, in his golf shop, on his kitchen surface, in the garage. I am sure I must have missed somewhere out!

This release was fabulous. I really needed this and I don't just mean from the sexual point of view. The hand holding, the cuddling up in bed, stroking my hair. All this, I had been denied. I needed it!

J U L Y   2 0 0 4

The house sale was almost complete after tremendous mistakes from the estate agent handling the sale, due to not adequately checking out the details of the chain involved. The agent had previously informed me that I was not allowed to know who was purchasing the house as he was very famous so I told her that if she didn't tell me his name then he wouldn't be able to purchase the house.

Therefore I decided to speak directly with Tony, who was purchasing our home and we had a good laugh along the way during a very stressful completion process. We decided to liaise with each others solicitors as, due to the agent's incompetence, the day of the completion had arrived, but no one moved anywhere. Tony was waiting to move in, all the contents of our house were packed up and in two removal vans on the drive and the house I was moving to had not been told that today was completion day. Also the man buying Tony's house didn't have his funds in place.

I simply couldn't believe that after all the stress there was more happening with no end in sight. When were things going to be plain sailing? The removal men then had to put some furniture back in the house for me and another ten days passed before the completion and move took place.

Tony and I were both furious that we had packed up our homes only for the move to fall apart and said that ironically he had been approached by a film production company shortly before asking if they could film his house move. He had declined but now said that he wished hadn't as this sorry escapade would have made good viewing. "What will you do now?" Tony asked, watching his removal vans driving back to his house and my removal vans stationary on the drive surrounded by all his garden pots and urns which be both decided was a good idea to leave there.

"No idea," I replied. "I thought I would be unpacking boxes now in my new home!" "Ditto! Well my girlfriend will be devastated by the news as she is waiting to lock up our home and drive here. Do you fancy coming back with me so we can all have some champagne?"

"I'd love to and we can have a laugh and sort this all out and arrange the completion ourselves."

One evening, at this was all going on, Deborah, my sister decided to impart some information to me which I really wish she hadn't. Clearly she thought that as my divorce was almost finalized this would no longer matter and I wouldn't care. But I did care very much.

Deborah has a strong spiritual side to her and believes very much in the eternal soul, but she also possesses a shoot to kill approach with her delivery style of her information and opinions.

She says it is blindingly obvious with a woman's intuition to spot the signs of a husband having an affair and that she would always be wise to it and would pick up on the signs. I suppose deceit is easier to spot when you are deceitful yourself. I am still not sure if her intention was to hurt me or to land Peter into an embarrassing situation as a revenge for his dislike of her. Quite where she thought her relationship with Joanne, her twin, would go after this, I am not sure she had considered the implications of which now that Joanne had prized her rich boyfriend away from his wife and children. Anyhow, she achieved all three.

"You must have worked it out by now," she started, "Peter and Joanne."

"What? What are you talking about?"

"Well why do you think she kept on coming round to your house all the time when Smithy left her?"

"Tell me now, what happened? They had an affair?" I felt sick. My husband and sister. That's disgusting. An affair is bad enough but with my sister! I was ashamed that two people so close to me had been behind my back like this.

Deborah went on to explain that around the time of my appointment with my divorce solicitor in 1993, when Joanne had looked after the children for me, Joanne decided that if I didn't want Peter, then she would have him. She reasoned that she could step into my shoes in my home and take over. It was a simple plan which she thought she would have no trouble in achieving. She saw the large house, the Mercedes and the Jaguar on the drive, the expensive holidays and clothes and she thought that she deserved this life even if I didn't want it. I cannot fathom where she had considered where I might fit into these plans.

There was worse to come. After Henry's death when Joanne's visits became ever more frequent with me thinking that it was because of her concern for me, although I had not now pursued a divorce, she was still plotting.

She wanted my perfect life of luxury that she saw as the primary aim for a woman. There was no perfect life, nothing is perfect, but there was money. No hard work to get there, just take someone else's life due to the fact that your own hasn't turned out quite how you would like. What you need in life to be happy is luxury and no money worries, was Joannes' ideal life.

Deborah claimed that she had said to Joanne how wrong she felt this was with my being her sister but Joanne said that she needed to get into this situation fast before another woman did. That's quite ironic really that it wasn't Joanne who got there in the end but the mystery woman whose false name of Deanna had now materialized into a real life name of Andrea and she too had form with married wealthy men. So the folklore of the Edgbaston ladies' set and the Metro bar gossip chattered.

"I am surprised that you didn't notice," Deborah continued, "I certainly would have if it had have been me. I know how easily affairs can start, but if it's any consolation to you, then I don't think they had full sex. It was just snogging and a bit more, but I do know Joanne gave Peter a blow job in a black cab one night coming home from Birmingham. On the nights you were upset crying over Henry, they were outside in the garden."

I pressed for more details on this and realized that on one of Peter's disappearing nights when he hadn't returned home but had instead stayed at Joanne's house, I didn't buy his flimsy explanation that rather than staying in the taxi for a further ten minutes to get home, he had chosen to stop off for a drink with Joanne and her then estranged husband. This was just months after Henry's death whilst we were discussing having more children.

The children and I moved house and things were difficult due to space. The house was a lot smaller than they were used to and added to this, Jack changed his mind about living with his father and the day that me Hannah George and Fred moved in to the new house, Jack moved in with us.

Of course I was delighted with this but had to make a lot of changes internally to accommodate us all. We were all under each others' feet so much so, that I started house hunting for a larger home. I asked Peter for financial help due to the changed circumstances but he told me to fuck off.

Soon after we had moved in, Peter announced that he was taking the children on holiday for three weeks to the States. I was quite bereft thinking about how I would cope not seeing them for three weeks but off they set with the newly identified girlfriend in tow. The gravy train had started rolling for her.

The morning after the children had left, I considered that although I wasn't happy that they weren't here, my friend Di was coming over that afternoon to discuss the possibility of arranging a holiday together.

Di and I had only known each other a matter of weeks but we had hit if off straight away and become firm friends. She knows more than anyone how I feel and has seen it all and lived through it with me for the last ten years. Her support has been invaluable to me. The fact that she didn't know me when Henry was alive, is helpful in that she knows me now. This person that I am. The mother of five children, one of whom is dead. Not the person I once was.

Suddenly my thoughts were disturbed when I heard the postman at the door and the first of many exocet missiles over the coming years, dropped onto the doormat.

It was a letter from Peter.

This was one of the nastiest and angriest and abusive collection of writings I have ever had the misfortune to read. A vitriol of abuse towards me.

He was after revenge clearly and wanted to hurt me as I had hurt him by leaving him and bruising his ego. The aim was achieved and I burst into tears sitting on the bottom step of my stairs clutching my knees sobbing.

I immediately telephoned my cousin John with whom I had a close relationship, and is one of the best people I know aside from my good friend Mr McCormick, at deciphering and understanding peoples' true motives and emotions. Regardless of what they claim.

John was furious that I was so upset and ordered me to throw the letter away and never read it again. Peter didn't like John and John didn't like Peter.

"Can't you see?" he implored, "Peter has timed this to hurt you the most just as you know them babbies (John grew up in the Black Country) are flying above now going thousands of miles away for three whole weeks. He is a coward and a bully to strike like that. Now stop crying, that's giving in to him and exactly what he wants. He needs you to regret your decision to divorce and this is the only way he knows how. To be abusive and make you lose your self esteem. He's been chip chip chipping away at you for years and he has no intention of stopping. You need to wise up to this bab."

I felt better talking with John and after the crying had stopped and with me telling John that this typed letter was quite similar to the first long handwritten letter I had received the previous year, stating that all our success financially had been down to him and him alone. Basically I was a mental nutter and he was a paragon of virtue. Littered with spelling mistakes, I really did laugh out loud at his threat that if it was ever mentioned again by me anything about him and Joanne that he would sue me for 'liable'. I still have the letter. When I had asked Peter if there was any truth in Deborah's allegations, his response was that Joanne had come on to him. This was strange as Joanne's response was that Peter had come on to her.

When I showed the letter to Mr McCormick and relayed John's reaction to it which he agreed with, Mr McCormick asked me to consider that if Peter was as happy as he claimed, why on earth would he feel the need to write to me, his ex wife about it?

Except that I wasn't his ex wife. Peter would not apply for the decree absolute. After three months my solicitor said that it was obvious Peter still didn't want this divorce to proceed and we had to threaten applying for it and now counter claiming against his original petition.

I naively thought that I could now forge a new life for myself. Being divorced meant I could live my life according to me now I thought, but how wrong I was. This was just the start.

That afternoon after briefly discussing the letter with Di we chatted about holiday plans. I had presumed that Di had a week in Spain or Portugal lying on a beach in mind, but she had far grander ideas.

"Let's go to Vegas!" she suggested. This thought initially filled me with dread as I do not enjoy flying and long haul flights were an ordeal for me. Little flights to Paris were my ideal. But then a thought permeated that although I wouldn't see the children, I would be in the same country as them.

Many years of Peter going to Las Vegas for computer conventions hadn't ever piqued my interest, despite the descriptions he gave on each return.

However, Di boldly produced a free Virgin long haul flight ticket she had received, which she offered to share with me to reduce costs if we went now to the travel agents to book. I am easily led and she got her way I am pleased to say! We visited my old friend Guy, a travel estate agent, whose first wife Mandy had been a very good friend of mine but had died of breast cancer at the age of only twenty six.

Before Mandy died, she asked me to promise her that I would always still talk to her when she was dead. I have always kept this promise and when I am alone in my car, I often talk out loud to her and joke with her in the way we used to do. She had a fantastic sense of humour even in the dark days before her inevitable death. It was to be a few years later that I received a wonderful message from Mandy.

So there we sat in front of Guy in his office choosing which hotel to stay in. They all looked amazing but as Di had been on previous occasions, we went with her desire to stay at The Bellagio which I thought looked superb.

We had a wonderful holiday and it was a world away from the previous two years of stress, hurt, and bewilderment. It was good talking to the children even though they were in a different state in America, giving me a crumb of comfort that they weren't too far away.

Di and I lived in a fantasy world that week imagining our lives in the future and on one such day had a fake conversation with each other that I was getting married that afternoon in one of the chapels in the hotel. We discussed my hair being in an updo, with Di checking that I hadn't washed my hair that morning as recommended for updos and the finer details of my makeup and dress. The lady on the sun lounger next to us by the pool was having difficulty hearing all the details moving ever closer to listen as she clearly believed this fake story.

I suppose that Di's opening gambit of, "Are you nervous?" and my immediate reply of "Not too nervous really, but I guess that will kick in this afternoon," had convinced the lady this was a true story.

Di and I had immediately formed what I suspected to be a lifelong bond and this was the tonic I needed. We haven't ever been back to Vegas but we often say we must as that week was such fun. It is a fantasy land there.

Chapter 10

My father arrived early on a Wednesday morning to carry on fitting my new kitchen. As soon as he arrived, he showed me a letter my mother had written addressed to, "To whom it may concern." The letter described that she had gone down to the river and she could not take any more. Dad immediately went down to the ford across the river near his home and looked, but could see nothing. The ford was swollen due to torrential November rain, but today was clear and fairly bright, although crisp and cold. Dad then drove around to the other side of ford from Catherine de Barnes to Solihull to walk along the river path and see if he could see anything that way. This happened within an hour of him picking the letter up and also seeing my mother alive in the house.

Although this should have sent immediate shock waves into us, we were actually more intrigued as to why she should write a letter like this. The reason being, that for the previous twenty five years, she had frequently disappeared sometimes with, but often not, with an explanation. Her excuse always was the same, "she needed to find herself." She embellished this with how everyone had upset her and she didn't have the life she wanted and blamed my father for her unhappiness.

We decided to see what happened as the day panned out as

we were sure that we would hear from her soon. Therefore, my father carried on with the kitchen fitting and my friend Ann called round for a coffee. The letter was discussed but so used were we to my mother's disappearing acts, that we did not lay the significance on this letter that others might.

When my dad left, I said I was meeting my friend Di later in Birmingham but to call me with any news of my mum. He reassured me that he was sure she would either be in touch or be back later but he would call me nevertheless.

That night the children were staying at their father's home so I felt pleased that I was free of responsibilities, should dad call.

I met Di in Birmingham and we went to a bar for a drink before deciding where to go to eat. Whilst we were chatting, and as I explained about this letter my dad had shown me, my mobile phone rang. It was dad saying he had called several people to see if they had heard from mum and although none had, two friends John and Gill had insisted on calling the Police and were now at his home. The Police had responded immediately but dad said he was just calling to let me know and not to worry, but he would be in touch.

Di immediately said, "what do you want to do?" "Go to dad's," I said "sorry to leave before we have eaten." "No problem, I am coming with you, let's go," she replied, "I will follow your car as I'm not sure of the way."

We arrived at dad's to find a police presence there. Dad explained that after Gill's call, the Police said although now dark, even though it was only nearing 7pm in the evening, they would search the ford and the river. Within minutes of this, we heard the Police helicopter. All of us went outside. A Policeman standing outside the house said this had been deployed as it had a heat seeking sensor able to detect a body and they felt this was necessary.

In dad's house we were quite shocked. Were helicopters really this readily available? Clearly they were to Solihull Police, as I was to find out at a further juncture in time.

Eventually at past nine o'clock, a Police officer rang the bell and said that they had found nothing, but they would resume their search on foot at first light.

We were all relieved and to be honest a bit of "well I knew they wouldn't find her," permeated all our thoughts as we knew her past endeavours to garner attention, and we had therefore presumed this to be one of so many we had endured before. "She would be back soon," we all agreed.

I didn't feel guilt at this point as my mother had started telling me she wanted to kill herself when I was thirteen years of age. She often explained that her plan was to drive at speed down the M42 motorway and suddenly swerve and crash into one of the pillars. In between these outbursts of describing how she would like to end her life, she was often normal in behaviour so you could easily forget and push them to the back of your mind. Survival instinct kicks in with fear and a fair amount of denial too.

The following morning, I immediately drove to dad's house. The Police presence was there at the ford. I had a coffee with dad and my mobile rang to say that my youngest daughter Fred didn't have her swimming kit with her and please could I bring it before 11 am, as she was upset. I told dad I would go and do this and try to be back within an hour and a half as this was a 15 mile round trip. "Alright bab, you go and do that for Fred, I'll see you in a bit."

Upon my return to dad's, a policeman opened the door and looked at me. "Hello," I stuttered, "I'm Julie, this is my dad's house, what's going on?" He gestured for me to come in but didn't say anything. As I walked towards the kitchen where I knew my dad would be, the policeman walked in front of me and stood in the doorway.

Dad was sitting at the kitchen table doing a crossword. "Dad?" I enquired, I had only been gone for an hour and twenty minutes. He explained that forensics were on their way to search the loft and the garage as there were no clues to my mum's whereabouts and in the meantime he was under 'house arrest.' This lasted for several hours.

You just couldn't make any of this up. Although the Police were obviously taking this very seriously, we still believed that mum would arrive back as she had done so many times before.

The Police decided to deploy the use of the helicopter once more. As we heard the thundering noise above, we couldn't help some black humour by joking that mum would love all this fuss and attention. Later that evening, there was an appeal by the Police for information about her whereabouts on the local news with a recent photograph.

When I saw the photograph within the news bulletin, although it was a photograph I had seen before, that was the first moment I knew she was dead. There was something about a departed soul to it that I instinctively felt. It is not something you could quite put your finger on, just a searing realisation. But despite an intensive search by the Police, it still made no sense that mum had literally disappeared. The Police's local enquiries had returned no information and any reasoning as to where she was, seemed futile.

The following day, the Police presence was even greater. Clearly, as mum had said in her letter that she had gone to the river, this is where they believed they would find her.

As soon as I arrived home from taking the children to school, Dad was knocking my door. "Any news?" I asked. "No bab, I just need to get away for a while."

He explained that on top of the Police presence, various members of my mum's family and long forgotten friends had all turned up to scour the riverbank to 'help' the Police. He himself had telephoned other people who may have had contact from her but this drew a blank, even from the taxi driver she used regularly. No one had heard from her.

Dad was starting to become angry and so was I, that the suggestion being made by relatives was that we her immediate family were not out searching for her. On the contrary, dad had searched for her in the first instance and my own daughter had driven down there with a feeling of helplessness watching the police search. I myself had walked down there several times only to be told by the Police that there was no way my mum could have gone further down the river than where they were searching, due to fallen trees blocking the way.

We both agreed that the best option was to let the Police do their job and ignore any outside interference. After all, the Police helicopter had drawn a blank two days running following the river to where it goes under the motorway. At this point I didn't confide in dad my worst fears as I could gauge he was feeling this too, due to the distant look in his eyes.

After a few coffees, dad said he'd go back home for a while for a rest and something to eat as he hadn't eaten since the previous morning. "Ok dad, keep in touch, call me immediately there is any news."

Approximately thirty minutes after dad had left, there was a knock at my door and I presumed it was dad coming back. I opened the door to two detectives flashing their warrant cards. They asked me to confirm my name and if they could come in.

I gestured for them to follow me into the kitchen. The news was blunt and delivered at lightning speed. I don't know if this was a technique or just the style of this particular detective inspector but nevertheless, it was excruciatingly painful.

"We've found your mother. I am so sorry." Uncontrollable tears followed and once again now as I write, almost nine years later. So that was it then. She had finally done it. She had killed herself. The details trickled out slowly, but the fact was that mum had carried out her threat that she would one day kill herself.

I asked the Police if they would like a cup of tea. Realising how mad this sounds, when you are in acute shock a sort of auto pilot takes over. One detective said yes please to a cup of the tea, whilst the other politely declined. My hands were shaking so much as I was filling the kettle I am surprised that I didn't drop it.

Suddenly my thoughts turned to dad. "What about dad? Where is he? Have you told him?"

"No, we came here to see you first as we thought your dad might be here. He told one of our officers this morning he was coming to see you."

"Right I need to phone him, get him here, I can't tell him over the phone. Can I tell him?" I rushed all this out in nano seconds.

"Yes, course. Ask him to come here and we shall wait. Then we must think of other family members who need to be informed."

"Hello bab," said dad, "any news?" "The Police are here dad, they need to ask some questions, can you come here now?" Dad wasn't fooled by my subterfuge and immediately asked, "why, what's happened? Have they found her?"

"Dad just come here now, they need to speak with us both." "Alright bab I'm just eating a sandwich, I'll be there in a bit." Well at the end of the day, better to get this news that your wife of almost forty-two years has killed herself without hunger in the mix. The sad fact is that as human beings we still need to eat and sleep although both of these basic requirements, necessary for survival, prove immensely difficult at times like this.

I waited in the hall so that I could quickly get dad in the house as soon as he arrived. Rushing out to greet him on the drive with this, was not the way I wanted to break this dreadful news, so I attempted to steady myself. Dad was as yet unaware of what I had to inform him.

As I opened the door, dad asked, "What is it bab? Whose car is that?" gesturing to the car behind him. "It's the Police dad, they are in the kitchen, come in," I took a breath, "they've found her dad."

Dad just crumpled. He is a small man and this news of course devastated him. Listening to someone threatening to kill themselves countless times does not prepare you for the realisation that they have achieved their aim. "Oh my God," he said over and over and tears were streaming down his face. I put my arms around him and we sobbed together.

We then had to ask the Police to inform Joanne and Deborah. I had had no contact with Joanne since the revelation of her trysts with Peter and Deborah had clearly taken sides. Dad felt it was best for the Police to do this as he was now visibly shaking.

The children were all very upset and despite all the difficult times were all happy to be with me at the funeral. For this occasion, I even had an offer from their father to help out by collecting them after the funeral although he unsurprisingly stopped short of offering his condolences. This was the Peter I knew.

As my mother had started divorce proceedings against my father, she had a vulture divorce solicitor from the same firm continuously hounding me. In fact in my case, the hounding only stopped in 2012 after ten years, when I sent them a handwriting report produced by a forensic scientist containing evidence that Peter had forged my signature for pension loans.

We respectfully requested that the divorce solicitor should not attend my mother's funeral by writing to the senior partner. However, one of the mourners told me she was there.

It later transpired that upon receiving the news of mum's death from the two detectives, Joanne had immediately telephoned mum's divorce solicitor with the information and made an appointment to go and see her. At this juncture, mum's body was still in the river.

Joanne was aware as were we all, that mum had recently changed her will to exclude me. The fact that it was still a married couple's mirrored will seems to have been left out of the equation in Joanne's mind. She believed that as I had been disinherited, and that mum had clearly stated that Joanne and Deborah would be her beneficiaries, now that mum was dead, and I guess the fact that she had started divorce proceedings, she would soon be coming into some money.

She had made her position clear when her husband had left her and her three children without money, that she would always chase money opportunities be they a wealthy man or whatever other means, rather than working.

In fact at a meeting that me, dad, Joanne and Deborah had to discuss the funeral, Joanne boldly announced that all married men were there for the taking. Dad told her to be quiet but she carried on empowered with her red wine making us all listen to her game plan, outlining how easy it was.

Suddenly my mobile rang and it was my friend Llewela. I said I'd call her back but dad told me to go and take the call having seen my unease at Joanne's diatribe on the sanctity of marriage.

I naturally presumed Llewela had called to offer her

condolences as our children were at school together and I thought someone had told her. However, she hadn't heard. Llewela had suffered her own share of immense grief and heartache.

"Hi how are you?" she enquired, "Not too bad thank you," I replied. "I was wondering if you are free next Tuesday? " she pressed on, "There's a film premiere on in Birmingham about the life of Brian Jones, from The Stones and I've been invited to go and wondered if you would like to come with me?"

"Obviously you haven't heard about my mum." "No, why? What's happened?" I proceeded to explain what had happened and Llewela was obviously aghast and very upset. "I can't believe that I have just invited you to see a film about a bloke who drowns in a swimming pool and your mum has just drowned in the river. I am so sorry, please forgive me." "Don't be ridiculous, you didn't know! We haven't half had some bad luck between us haven't we?" I concluded, saying that I would speak to her again soon.

Dad told me I should go as a distraction, and spend an evening with my friend. So I did, and we shared some black humour that evening, that only people suffering extreme tragedy would understand. I saw an old friend of my parents' at the premiere who had in fact, given a speech on behalf of the guests at my wedding. He and his wife had heard the news and they said they knew mum would carry out her threat one day. They were terribly sorry and informed me that they already had the details of the funeral and would both be there.

Mum's room was so cold before her funeral, icily cold despite the central heating being on full blast. I asked the Vicar to come and see for himself and if there was anything he could do to help. He came round and me, dad, Joanne and Deborah stood in this freezing room although we had all felt the radiator with our hands which was boiling hot.

The Vicar said prayers for all of us and said that mum needn't be worried about staying here. No one was criticising her for what she had done.

The room became immensely hot no more than fifteen minutes later. We all felt the change. Mum was free, she didn't need to linger here any longer.

We were all very impressed and the Vicar modestly said he hadn't done much, but he had achieved a miracle as far as I was concerned.

Deborah suggested tentatively that her medium friend Michael should visit us all for some spiritual healing. Michael was good. Very good. He announced that mum wasn't sorry for what she had done and that she was never going to apologise. She was happy to be free and was having a drink with Joan, my aunt, John's mother watching us from the spirit world.

Michael then went around the table and very perceptively picked up on several surprising facts. When he turned his attention to me, he declared that I was to marry again in the future. I was more than surprised at this but he was insistent that I was to marry someone with dark looks who was very interested in history, particularly Greek history and that he currently lived in Plymouth. He also said that this person had a fascination with the sea which matched mine. Truthfully this sounded preposterous to me. I was going to marry someone from Plymouth? I didn't believe this for one moment.

Joanne didn't get very far with her quest for mum's money due to her negligence in not understanding the legality of a married couple's will. Everything now belonged to dad and mum's wishes died with her. It was up to dad now to write a new will.

Despite this, the solicitor had the temerity to send dad a bill for Joanne's appointment. Needless to say he didn't pay it and the fallout from this has been a distance which I do not believe will be resolved.

Chapter 11

We decided to bury mum's ashes on her sixtieth birthday and the vicar agreed for them to be in the churchyard near Henry's grave. Only the immediate family were there and a few friends. The situation was so awkward because of Joanne and there was a distinct parting of two camps after the little service performed outside by the Vicar. How embarrassing, but considering all that had happened, totally expected.

Life resumed for everyone, all rather deflated that mum's life had ended like this.

I was now nearing the opening of my shop, a franchise with the Italian fashion label, MaxMara and very excited. The plan was to earn enough to support me and the children without the constant monthly fear of that dreaded maintenance cheque not turning up. In 2006, no one could foresee the financial crash on the horizon.

The first eighteen months were great fun and exciting. This was the only time in the last few years that I didn't have to worry about money as I was earning my own. Working full time running the house and children by myself was exhausting but still I thought if you work hard, everything will turn out well.

I opened the shop with my friend Jan. We knew each other

through our sons being friends at school and she and I had become particularly close at the time of Henry's death. Jan accepted how different life was for me, and how I felt. She was very supportive of me when I needed peace, and didn't try and rush me to presume normal life activities outside of the routine of just living. When Peter had started the children's residence proceedings, she was outraged and understood his motives. She more than anyone had witnessed the verbal abuse I had suffered, and didn't accept his explanation that it was all said jokingly. When the court proceedings were happening, she came to court to support me and saw that I clearly hadn't eaten anything for a whole week and had lost a stone in weight. "If Peter gets custody of George and Fred, we will go to South America. You, me, George and Fred. We'll make a new life for ourselves. This is not on. Those children need to be with you. They need a mother more than they need a father. I won't let this happen." She said this with such conviction that I believed her. I shall always be grateful to her for that. I was devastated at Peter's actions.

The downside of having just one supplier for the merchandise in a shop is that you are totally beholden to them but once again I had been trusting of a situation only to be let down by their refusal to understand the effects of the recession on a small business. When I finally had to accept the inevitable and close the business down, I had been receiving daily telephone calls asking me to settle outstanding invoices and their unrelenting requests of "Julie, just pay," became quite comical as I didn't have the money, which I had patiently explained. The sales had virtually dried up overnight. Everyone was cutting back and a large proportion of small businesses were the first casualties. Large high street stores followed suit. However, I was currently a riding a wave of good income and was able to provide for the children in the manner to which they had become accustomed.

Nicky, a lady who worked for me in the shop asked me to attend a meeting with her where a visiting clairvoyant would give individual readings. I did not feel the need to keep on trying to contact Henry's spirit through mediums as I didn't feel that is was a good idea for him or for me. As far as I was concerned, I had my irrefutable proof that one day my soul would be with him again and this pain of him not being here with my other children would go.

Mandy Honey was an unusual lady in that she spoke fairly quickly about situations in which you were going to find yourself in the future, in a matter of definitive fact. She wrote everything she was saying down with the instruction of, "keep these notes and tick them off as you go along and each event happens." The cynic in me was very awake.

I didn't speak at all but handed her my watch to hold as she requested. She immediately said that one of my children was in spirit but all of my other children were coping well and were happy. She had nothing more to say regarding Henry, other than we need to let things happen within our destiny and act accordingly. She also stated that I had a parent in spirit, but offered no further information.

I have kept her notes and I am astounded to inform you that almost all of the events have since happened. She told me I would soon be going to Canada and drew a small picture of the Canadian flag, where I would meet lots of French speaking relatives. This was laughable to me at the time. She also said that I would soon start dating a man living rurally with lots of horses. This happened two years later and the man cared for retired race horses.

Mandy was very concerned about documents, explaining that there was lots of betrayal going on against me and I needed to watch my back. "Do not sign anything," she urged. Sadly I forgot about this message and ignored it entirely. She also said that my business would fail although it transpired that this didn't happen immediately.

She said that I would be moving a long way away in the future and would find more calm for my troubled soul. My fascination with the sea was picked up on and she declared that I had drowned in a former life. She said that this etched into my soul was not a worry for me and didn't frighten me.

My dad doesn't always look after himself with eating healthily and she picked up on this and told me to tell him and questioned his fascination with a watch. He kept his deceased mother's watch on his bedroom cupboard. He really loved his mother.

She said that I would become a grandmother within the next seven years and that it would be twins. This was the only detail she got wrong as seven years later Hannah made me a grandmother with her beautiful daughter Penelope. Just one baby, not twins.

Mandy said a few other general things which I didn't particularly pick up on specifically but ended with, "you have a friend in spirit called Mandy and she will talk to you soon, but now is not the right time." So my Mandy had been listening to me then all these years, just as I had suspected.

"Life is all about timing, and following our instinct so go and enjoy your life, remembering to tick everything off as you go along. It will all happen, I promise you."

Chapter 12

I received an extremely rare, friendly telephone call from Peter asking me if I had booked a flight to Germany for Joerg's wedding, and if I had any details on the accommodation available. Peter was on a break from his girlfriend at this time.

Joerg had been a friend of mine since I was thirteen. A family holiday to Ibiza in August 1978, and a chance encounter in a swimming pool between me and my two sisters and two German brothers, resulted in a lifelong friendship between me and Joerg. So close were we, that he flew over for Henry's funeral arriving a couple of days early to spend time supporting us, but refusing our hospitality of staying with us as he had done many times in the past. He came with me to the florist to arrange the flowers for Henry's funeral. Peter was at the opening of the inquest into Henry's death that day, and he had steadfastly refused my wish to go, saying that as a formality, I didn't need the distress. I had mixed feelings about this, but the sad and irrefutable truth was that whatever happened nothing was going to bring Henry back. In fact he had lived with us for a while in 1989, as he came to England to improve English and worked for us in the business for two years. He was devastated about Henry and only weeks before, had stayed with us for a few days with his lifelong friend Oliver and Maren, Oliver's wife.

Oliver was a very keen photographer and had taken many photographs of the children and all of us enjoying ourselves on days out to Warwick Castle and other local attractions during their stay. These photographs became a lifeline for me after Henry's death as they were so different to the hundreds that I had taken of Henry, as these were much more professional, but not posed for. Stunning captures of a little child with his parents, brother and sister and close friends. Playing, laughing, eating, drinking his bottle. In January, 1994, Oliver sent a special delivery parcel to me. Inside was a special book Oliver had made with all the photographs. I fell to the floor to sit and look through the book and was so grateful for the effort he had made. His intention was clearly to make this book anyway as a thank to us for our hospitality, but the emphasis now on the photographs with Henry in them was apparent, and he had clearly worked hard on presenting this to me. I was very grateful and sent him a note thanking him. This book has been thumbed through millions of times.

I first met Oliver on a visit to Joerg in Wiesbaden in 1980 when I was fifteen. He was so handsome and I felt so nervous around him I became quite quiet in his company. Joerg is also very handsome but although we did plenty of teenage snogging and a little bit more, our relationship has always been platonic. My German language skills were quite good then, and I went on to study A level in the subject. This was very handy as Oliver spoke little English whereas Joerg was extremely keen to improve his. At this point I am sure that Joerg wouldn't mind me saying that my German skills were superior to his English. However, mine through non practice, are woefully inadequate now compared to his fluent English.

We went out many times as a threesome, on this visit of mine with me riding either on the back of Joerg's or Oliver's motorbike. I never did tell my parents that I had been on the back of a motorbike, as they wouldn't have allowed it.

One particular day, we were going out to play crazy golf and Joerg suggested that I ride with Oliver for a change. My heart was fluttering like mad! Getting on to the back of his motorbike and wrapping my arms around him was heaven! In fact he took a few sharp bends rather precariously, but I didn't worry. I just took the opportunity to hold on to him even more.

When we stopped, Joerg asked if everything was ok, and I said yes fine. Oliver and Joerg then continued with a fast exchange of conversation in German which I pretended to understand. Although I generally got the gist of conversations even if I didn't understand all the words, when they spoke quickly, I soon lost the thread.

They were laughing because Oliver thought I was frightened of being on the back of his bike as he drove faster, instead of Joergs', when in actual fact nothing could have been further from the truth! I loved being on that bike with him. In fact I just wanted to be with him! Anyhow, living in separate countries at the ages we were, there was not much chance of anything happening between us, even though we did see each other on further visits I made to Germany.

I explained to Peter which flight I was taking, and that I had booked a room at the hotel where the wedding and the reception was taking place. He was surprised and asked how I knew that there was accommodation available at the venue. I explained that I had e mailed Joerg and asked him. It is hardly rocket science. Peter then said that he was on a different flight to me as he had left it too late to book and asked if I would be wearing the clothes I would be wearing to the wedding on the plane, or getting changed there. Gosh, he really did need hand holding although not in the literal sense of course. Peter was unable to book a room at the wedding venue as it was now fully booked.

I was very excited to go to Joerg and Lillie's wedding even though it was going to be a short trip staying only one night. Sometimes, one night can be spectacular. For all sorts of reasons.

The hotel was located in a beautiful woodland setting outside of Wiesbaden. When I arrived, the staff were clearly preparing for the wedding and there was no sign of anyone else around. I double checked with the receptionist that I was in the right place as suddenly I felt a panic that it was odd that I should be the first one to arrive. There was no problem she assured me that I was definitely in the right place and the groom was expected shortly.

Therefore, I went to my room and showered and changed for the wedding. The positive side of owning a dress shop, is being able to choose from the latest collections and I was very pleased with the black and cream striped Sportmax skirt and jacket I was wearing. I was pleased I looked good. As I sat at the dressing table at the open window, applying my make up, I heard male voices outside. I stood up and looked out to see Joerg and another man chatting and laughing. "Guten Tag!" I called from my window. "Die Julie! Wie gehst? Komm her!" replied Joerg. I wondered who the other man could be as I had presumed that Oliver would have been Joerg's best man. I didn't recognize this man.

As I walked outside to Joerg I immediately realized that the other man was Oliver! The reason for me not recognizing him after fourteen years, was that he had lost a lot of hair and was wearing glasses, but as soon as I saw his face and more importantly his eyes, he looked the same.

A few choruses from the two of them of "Die Julie!" and "sie sieht aber gut aus!" "Ja sie sieht gut!" "Sehr gut", from Oliver (I understood the she looks good bit!), and hugs and kisses all round as they continued in German with me understanding little but with Joerg translating as he knew my German now was not what it was. Oliver presumed I could understand more than I could and offered no English at all, just the same as twenty seven years previously!

Gradually the wedding guests started to arrive. Soon, I saw Peter. "Hi," I ventured. "Hi, where's Joerg?" he enquired. Joerg was chatting to other guests so it was left for me and Peter to stand together. This was awkward at first due the amount of animosity and hostility which had been created in the divorce. But here we stood, side by side chatting in a way we hadn't for many years. Clearly the situation was all the easier as neither of us had anyone else there and we were virtually the only English guests and Peter doesn't speak any German. When we did chat with other guests, one asked if we were married and Peter replied that we used to be, but that we had five children together and that neither of us had children with anyone else.

Joerg's family duly arrived and hugs and kisses from his parents Ewald and Lore and his brother Marc. Everyone remembered me speaking decent German in years gone by so they all expected me to still understand whilst they all spoke at a speed I didn't remember. Anyhow smiles all round and we were awaiting the arrival of the bride. This was the first time I had met Lillie. She was lovely and told me how happy she was to meet one of Joerg's oldest and most special friends.

Joerg explained to me after the ceremony that he had arranged for me and Peter to sit on different tables for the wedding breakfast, as he knew how awkward this might be for us. Peter was disappointed when he discovered this and wondered if it were possible to change this. I said to leave things as they were. What I was hoping for was to sit near to a recently divorced Oliver.

The meal was typically Germanic which I enjoy, and I chatted to lots of interesting people some I had met many years before. There was a fantastic rendition in German to the tune of "Ring of Fire" performed by Joerg's friends with substituted words along the lines of Joerg finally making it down the aisle. The atmosphere was fantastic and everyone was very relaxed and happy. Dancing followed and I danced with Oliver.

As soon as the meal was over, people started going outside for air or to smoke. I went outside. Peter and Joerg were standing smoking large cigars with their drinks resting on a large old wooden beer barrel. "Here she is," said Peter, "come and have a drink with us bab, what would you like?" I looked at their glasses of red wine and said I'd like the same please.

Peter went inside to fetch the drinks and Joerg told me how happy he was to have found Lillie and that he was pleased Peter and I could be civil with one another and that he hoped it would continue. He also said he was sorry we weren't together and things had turned out the way they had. Peter arrived back with the drinks and put his arm around me. At this point I momentarily flinched as this was a million miles away from the last five year's antics. Peter's arm remained around my shoulder for a while longer.

A friend of Joergs' whom I knew vaguely joined us and upon seeing this, exclaimed how happy he was to see Peter and me back together again. Joerg quickly explained in German that we were not back together but his friend protested that he could still see something there between us and urged me to do something about it. When the dialogue was explained to Peter, he said "I'll always love Julie, and she knows it."

We all carried on chatting and laughing and Oliver came to

join us still believing that I could understand German now as well as I used to be able to. However, I just loved hearing him talk and at the end of the day, the look of lust or love has a complete language of its' own.

Soon, a taxi arrived and Peter declared it was time for him to go. I said it had been nice seeing him and to have a safe trip back. "I'm staying at the Nassauer Hof where we always used to stay, come with me?" was Peter's opening gambit. I laughed and smiled. "I'm serious, come with me?" he asked with a cheeky grin. This was bizarre. I had been to hell and back over the divorce and was emotionally spent from years of pain, grief, and torment. And now, he wanted me to go to his hotel with him, five years after we had separated! "Thanks, but no thanks," I said, "I'll speak to you soon." "Don't be afraid, no funny business, I promise," was his last attempt, as he started to get into the taxi, "come on! Be brave."

As I stood there, all I could feel was the absurdity and irony of the situation after everything that had happened. As Peter's taxi drove away, Peter shouted out of the window, "if you change your mind, you know where I am, and it's room 117." That's the technique the cheeky charmer had used to woo me when I was seventeen by declaring that I should call him on Littlewick Green 225, insisting that I do the chasing. I refused then to this tactic and still we ended up together for twenty years but I refused now, as I knew it wouldn't work. It couldn't. This was so sad, I thought.

As I turned to walk back into the hotel, Oliver was in front of me. He asked me in German if I would like to go for a walk. Oh yes I would very much like to go for a walk with you tonight Oliver I thought. "Ja," I replied, "danke."

As we started walking into the garden in front of the hotel, Oliver took my hand. The night was full of stars, so many stars that I don't think I have ever since seen a night sky like it. Oliver explained his love of astronomy and although I couldn't decipher all the German words, I got the gist. As he was pointing out the stars and naming some of them, he stopped at one and mentioned Henry's name. I felt huge emotion but didn't cry as I knew that Oliver's words were to comfort me, and it was his way of saying how sorry he was.

I was enjoying this attention so much, that I didn't want this night to end. Without any explanation, after about an hour we went into the hotel and Oliver followed me up the stairs.

There was not much sleep that night, just talking all night long and kissing. Nothing else, talking and kissing. My German was so poor now but we muddled along and understood each other very well. We talked about the meaning of life in broken English, German but mostly eye contact. Oliver held me all night.

Chapter 13

Two months after this, completely out of the blue, my dad suggested that I go to Canada with him and his brother as his Aunt Nell would be a hundred years of age and there was to be a big party for her. Wow I thought, Mandy Honey was right. Never in my life had I considered going to Canada and now I was. Great aunt Nell was my grandfather's sister.

Ottawa is an extremely large city and Tony my uncle, wasn't the best driver in the world, so it was going to be interesting to see how we found our way to the hotel where we were to be staying, and the party was to be held. As we drove into Carling Avenue, Tony declared that he remembered that this was very close to the apartment block where Aunt Nell lived. He pulled into a side road leading to a hotel and said "let's ask that bloke in the funny hat if he knows where our hotel is," to a man walking towards our rented car.

"Hello mate," he started, "can you tell us where the Macies hotel is please?" The man looked into the car at Tony, Dad and then me, sitting in the back. I wondered what the delay was in him speaking.

"Tony, Ronnie, Julie, I don't believe it! " He took off his hat and Tony recognised him as his second cousin, Mark. I had met him many years before when he had visited England but I didn't recognise him as he had lost a lot of hair. I seemed to be making a habit of this.

We had travelled for virtually ten hours and the first person we see and speak to is a relative.

It was so wonderful to arrive at my Great Aunt Nell's apartment to find her making herself boiled eggs and bread and butter at almost one hundred years of age. She was very sprightly and not so unchanged from the last time I had seen her more than twenty years before. She insisted that we all sit down and had a gin and tonic with her which was her favourite tipple.

When I told her that I had started writing a book mainly about my experiences after Henry's death, she pulled out a photograph she had of him she kept in her diary which my mother had sent to her. "That's a good idea," she said, "but get along and write it quickly as I would like you to write a story about my life and my journey to reach here." I laughed, and said that I would think about it and see how I got on with this first, but she insisted that I take some notes now before she died declaring that she didn't want to live forever, just another ten years would be fine.

I already knew the bare bones of her story of course but I shall try to keep to my promise to her and write her story when I finish mine. My great grandmother had sold Nell to the gypsies for a bag of sugar in 1914 so the social services of the day had taken Nell, Jack my grandfather and their sister Ivy into care and placed them with the nuns. An opportunity arose for children to decide if they wanted a new life in Canada. My grandad declined but Nell and Ivy chose to go and there is now a vast Canadian arm to the family, some of them, French speaking. Their father, my great grandfather had been killed in action in the first world war.

As we had signed a fifteen year lease on the shop with five yearly break clauses, and were only two years into it, it made sense to try to run the shop as an independent boutique with far less overheads and commitments. The hope was there and despite hard work and a very promising start, there was no other option but to close down. The recession was taking hold fast.

I had hoped that due to our conversation at Joerg's wedding that Peter and I could be civil and I telephoned him and explained the difficult business situation I was in. He was aware that he had never paid maintenance for all four children and that I was struggling, but he knew that I wouldn't take the matter to court through lack of funds. He gave me a cheque for £3000 to help out with the words of warning, "this is to help you, not for you and Jan to go drinking champagne in the Metro bar."

He held a grudge towards Jan and to my sister Deborah which he had clearly outlined in a handwritten nineteen page letter he had sent to me in 2002. The letter was full of denial that he had played any part in the marriage breakdown, but that it was clearly Jan and Deborah who had persuaded me to go for a divorce and it was their fault that I had listened to their advice. Everyone I know was shocked to hear the news of our divorce and had thought we had the perfect marriage. We did have a perfect family with a member missing, but we did not have a perfect marriage.

Peter's grudge against Jan had deepened when he learned that she had reported to me seeing Peter keep ending calls from me to his mobile whilst he was drinking in her restaurant when sometimes I was frantic with worry for his whereabouts. He loved winding me up and playing games.

One particular incident, was very distressing during the

divorce proceedings. I received a telephone call from Jan asking me if I was alone. "Yes," I replied, "Peter is collecting the children today from school."

"I think you are going to be really shocked," she started, "in fact I'm so shocked myself, I don't know where to start. It's taken me a while to collect my thoughts and call you."

She went on to say that Peter had telephoned her earlier claiming that he urgently needed her help. He clarified that Jan was at the time my closest friend and therefore she would certainly want was best for me. Obviously Jan agreed, curious as to where this was leading.

"It is so obvious that Julie is mental and has clearly lost her mind in wanting this divorce." "Peter, Julie is very unhappy and that is why she wants a divorce." "No, no no I'm not having that, we are a very happy family." "Yes I know that," agreed Jan, "but Julie is not happy with the marriage."

Peter was having none of this and then said he had looked into getting me committed to a mental home where I could rest and recuperate and get rid of this ridiculous idea of having a divorce.

"You know how unstable she is Jan," Peter implored, "the best thing is if you and I sign the paperwork and we get her committed until she feels better."

"Julie is not unstable, she is unhappy and that is it." It takes a lot to get Jan worked up, she is a calm and placid person, but she was starting to become angry now. "It is a pity that you haven't listened to Julie before and this constant piss taking you do of her, isn't funny. Other people don't find it funny."

Peter was angry now as he had felt sure he could convince Jan to be his partner in crime to get me declared insane. Clearly this tactic failed but it did not stop Peter's attempt at labelling me mad to anyone who would listen.

Despite these past events, I thanked Peter for the money and assured him I really did need the money for the children and that it would not be spent on champagne. With Jan in the Metro bar.

Shortly after this, Peter telephoned me to say that there had been a bit of a mix up with a forgotten company pension plan and it was nothing to be worried about or get excited about, but he needed my signature and there would be, "£11,000 coming your way. If it's ok with you I will send David my financial advisor round with some papers for you to sign. You like David don't you?" I didn't suspect a thing. No alarm bells rang. No horn was sounded. Peter had me in the net. It was as easy as that. I remained a trusting person despite the trauma I had been through and wrongly presumed that because I didn't go out conning people, I wouldn't be openly conned myself. Smiling cheerful assassins are the ones to be feared.

Peter also informed me that the business was doing really well and that he had hit the big time. "What a shame for you that you divorced me at the wrong time," he laughed. "I shall soon be a multi millionaire."

I believed that since the time at Joerg's wedding, there was an improvement in relations between Peter and I so much so that I thought it would continue to grow. Clearly still very naive at tactics, I thought no more of this pension malarky until David came to my home with a fairytale to tell.

"Don't tell Peter that I have told you this but you don't have £11,000 to invest, but £50,000!" That was a nice round figure wasn't it? Still I fell for it even though I questioned why this wasn't sorted out in the divorce. After all hadn't David sent a printout to my solicitor of pensions totalling significantly smaller amounts than this? This was different he explained, the company plan had to stay in the company until now but the pension rules had changed and this is why the money had to be put into individual pensions. Really struggling for money at this point, I enquired if I could have the money now. No, David explained that it had to go into a pension plan in my name. Also as luck would have it, David had done some research on my behalf and he just so happened to have all the paperwork for me to sign. That was so kind of him. He laid the paperwork out in a horizontal fan. These were my new equities in various stocks and bonds he clarified. How the plotters must have laughed! I signed the papers in front of me.

There was no mention of loans being taken out in my name being finally repaid, but he did say that as some loans had been repaid, the fund needed now to be closed down. Funnily enough, the reason why I didn't know about the loans was because I didn't sign the loan agreement documents which were taken out in my name. I didn't question it further. If you don't know something, you don't know it.

I soon forgot about this, as David had explained that I couldn't draw on this pension until I was fifty five years of age.

As the year rolled on and money was becoming much scarcer with the shop barely breaking even, I continued to receive letters from Peter's solicitor every time there was an argument in the house or any sort of disagreement, particularly with me disciplining the children. I had grown so tired of many of Peter's words coming out of the childrens' mouths and when I started pointing this out to them, they didn't like it. Many fathers and indeed mothers use the children as foot soldiers to convey a message to the other parent.

There was a mole in the other camp who regularly updated me on the master plan and that I should be very wary. The mole informed me that Peter was openly discussing how he was not going to carry on paying maintenance to me for the children, and that he was persuading the younger two to live with him in his new big house which would have a tennis court and swimming pool. The older two had left home at this stage, so they were free to do as they pleased.

I didn't really believe that we would have to go through all that again but the mole was entirely correct. The younger two were being worked on. "Trust me," the mole said, "I've heard the way they are being spoken to."

The six years living on my own with the children involved a lot of staying in. I never employed a baby sitter choosing only to go out socializing when the children stayed with their dad. My bed was frequently their bed too.

However, I was heavily criticised for having a boyfriend especially one eleven years younger than me and he only stayed one night at the house in four years. The children described this as outrageous and they were not going to tolerate it. When I pointed out that their dad had a girlfriend, they explained to me that that was different as he was their dad but as their mum I needed to be there just for them. This came from the younger two predominantly. Fred liked Richard, my boyfriend, but George didn't. Hannah and Jack were getting on with their own lives.

When I closed the shop, Deborah asked me to come and work for her cleaning company. I had no option now to do this although I didn't particularly like it, I needed an income fast.

Peter telephoned me and said that he would help me out in the half term holidays whilst I was doing my cleaning jobs, and have the children for a couple of days. I said that it was fine thanks as I had booked them into a children's holiday club at the gym.

That conversation took place on the Tuesday. On the Sunday he came to the house when I had gone out for one hour to meet my new boyfriend for a drink, with the older two in charge and took George and Fred at fourteen and twelve to live with him for good. They were all going to live happily ever after without me. I was finally well and truly persona non grata. It would be better if I was air brushed out of history completely.

The first telephone call I made was to my saviour, Mr McCormick explaining that he'd finally carried out his threat. "Come and see me on Tuesday, I have an appointment slot at ten in the morning."

There was really no surprise to be had here when you considered that Peter had been relentless in his claim that everything the marriage had created was his. The business, the money, the children. One voicemail he left on my mobile stated, "if the child has my name, then it belongs to me." I think he should realise that no one belongs to anyone. Ever. We are all our own individual beings.

Mr McCormick discussed everything through with me regarding my options, and suggested that I just give in to the situation and that it was inevitable that it had come to this. All the threats for years, were just biding time...

He had been aware of every twist and turn in this tale due to my regular sessions with him, and it was so easy for him to have a bird's eye view having listened to Peter with his own ears. He said many times that Peter did not behave like a middle class white businessman. On the contrary he had a Muslim man's attitude towards women and children. Mr McCormick said, "you are still their mother, and you don't have to live with the children to be a good mother."

I was naturally devastated at this turn of events but there was nothing I could do. The children wanted to live with Peter and I was informed that there was no coercion involved. My mole said, "I told you so."

Financially I was in a mess no longer receiving a maintenance, which was typically in arrears, with a large house and a large mortgage. Putting the house up for sale received ridiculous offers on it at the height of the recession. I had to think of another way as the cleaning work wasn't bringing in enough to survive on and pay the bills.

So I took the decision to take in lodgers.

This was very very difficult. Suddenly I had to share my home with strangers. Mentally I was now so exhausted that I seriously wondered how much more I could cope with. I don't mean to follow my mother down the suicide route, but all I had wanted was a happy quiet nice life. This one had been too full of trauma, drama and pain. Goodness only knows about all of my previous lives and what was to follow in the future! That didn't bear thinking about, I most certainly didn't want to come back for another life when this one ends. Stop the world, I want to get off, became my mantra in my head.

Shortly after this I received a strange request from Chris, Peter's business partner. He had sent a with compliments slip in the post with a document for me to sign to close down a company pension fund of which he, Peter and I were the trustees. This document listed the percentages of the shares in this fund and mine was the lowest. Finally the light came on for me. Something had been going on behind my back.

I telephoned a friend who had been involved in a large computer business and asked her what she thought. "For goodness sake," she implored, "do not sign it, you need to find out what's been going on. I shall call my financial advisor who is a pensions' expert and see if he can call you with advice."

Les, duly called and asked me to explain the picture I was now presented with. He advised me to immediately call the pension company and ask for copies of these loans. This will be at the heart of it he assured me and he also informed me that he was aware of my divorce solicitors' failings when it came to pensions. She never looked into them simply presuming that any evidence presented to her was factual. It was every businessman's chance to wriggle out of a full and correct financial settlement when they had company pensions and they retained all the documents.

These documents duly arrived a few weeks later, having had to be dug out of the archives. I looked at the documents and surprise surprise even though my name was clearly on the dotted line, the signatures bore no resemblance to my real signature. I could clearly see that Peter had forged by signature. Well, when I say forged, I mean attempted to, as the likeness was extremely poor. The loans were for tens of thousands of pounds dating back to 2002.

So began a journey of being met with a brick wall when I demanded an explanation from Peter and Chris. Instead of talking with me, they used bullying tactics and I was not going to ever give in to those. I had morals even if they didn't, and I was incandescent when I realised I had been conned. When David had come to my home with his fairytale, he had slipped in a document which he told me was for a new pension but it was the start of the closing down process of the fund. However, the fund remained open and they needed my signature, which I steadfastly refused to give. They had received terrific returns on the money with the company now turning over £56 million a year. I wanted a share and was furious at being deceived like this.

Some Edgbaston ladies I had known from when the children were younger invited me to have a dinner with them in Solihull. One of them in particular Joanna, had been a very good friend when Henry died. They knew the children were now with Peter and were very supportive of how difficult this must be. I also told them about the forgeries.

I revealed to them that I had started writing a book about my life and the difficulties I had faced. They all immediately thought this a wonderful idea and asked my main motive for writing. I explained my primary motive would be cathartic, and I certainly would like to help others in a bereaved situation like mine, but if I made some money from it, then all the better. They then flattered me by saying that they thought it would be a success and someone would buy the film rights. One said that Demi Moore could play me and another said Catherine Zeta Jones. I protested they had too much faith in me. One asked if there would be any sex in the book as people loved reading about sex. I said there'd be a sprinkling and she advised me to put more in.

I also had lunch with Richard, my conveyancing solicitor at this time, who has become a good friend and he had been very helpful giving me some free advice on selling the shop lease. Treating him to lunch was the least I could do.

I told Richard that I had started writing a book as I felt that alongside being something I had always wanted to do, I had a story to tell which was sad, uplifting at times I hoped, about a struggle to carry on sometimes. I was concerned with all the trouble which had occurred, that I would get threatened with legal action for laying my own soul bare due to the obvious references I had to make to what had happened and the other people involved. For this reason, I considered changing the names of all concerned and telling my story as fiction.

Richard thought this was a bad idea to change the names of those involved, and suggested I speak to a publisher about this. "People love stories about other peoples' lives Julie, let them get into your head. I think it's a great idea, go on and finish it!" Well six years after that lunch, I am almost there. On the final furlong.

The publisher's advice was that if I was telling a true story then it was essential that I used everyone's correct names. So I have.

My eldest daughter had visited a spiritualist at this time and was happy that she had had messages from her deceased grandfather and my mother.

I told Di I was planning to book an appointment and she suggested that I book one for her too and that we could go out for lunch afterwards to discuss our experiences.

The large modern detached house where Pearl lived, belied the woman living there. She had long black hair and a gypsy style outfit wearing several strands of colourful beads. A tiny bit of cynicism existed in me. The house and the person just didn't match. Pearl explained that she had a gift of communicating with spirits which had been passed on from her own mother, when she had passed over into the spirit world. She saw spirits all around. As if she sensed my doubting thoughts, she explained that her husband was a businessman who travelled away often so she had freedom to give readings and allowing the spirits to come to her and communicate as and when. She followed this by stating that her husband was a non believer but they existed in perfect harmony, allowing each other their own paths and destinies.

Di had her reading first whilst I sat drinking a cup of tea in another room.

When Di came out she looked at me in a non impressed way to suggest that her reading hadn't been quite what she had hoped, so I went in without too much expectation.

As soon as I sat at the small round table opposite Pearl in her study, Pearl looked up at the blank wall next to us and put her hands over her ears and commanded, "Stop! Stop all of you. I cannot listen if you are all talking at once."

This was like being in a film where you knew something was going to happen, but not what, and still the cynic in me remained.

Pearl explained that she could see an array of family and friends in the room who all wanted to talk to me. I asked her who she could see and she started with my paternal grandmother who she correctly named as Catherine. She also named Jack my grandfather, my uncle Graham, my mother Jackie sitting with my aunt Joan, (my cousin John's mother), my father in law, Eddie, Dolly, my maternal grandmother, and a Bill or a William whose name I didn't recognize, but who had been mentioned to me before as my guardian angel. She said that a Chris from the past would come into my life and this was to be a change of direction for me.

Tears were rolling down my cheeks now as she could not possibly have known all these names. "They are so happy to see you and want you to know how much you are loved. You must stop worrying."

The finale was even better. "I have Mandy here and she loves you so much, and is so grateful that you have talked to her for all of these years just like you promised that you would." By now, I was sobbing, but the best was yet to come.

"Mandy is holding hands with a little boy. I don't think he's little now but this is the image I see of him before he passed over. He is wearing denim dungarees with a checked cap on. I'm not sure of his name but I think it's Harry. Mandy says surely you must have known that she would look after him for you." Pearl then said that an Aunty Vi had been there for Henry's passing into the spirit world but that Mandy had soon taken over to look after him.

Well at this point I may as well have been on the floor I was crying so much, all the time not saying anything, just listening.

Pearl asked me if I wanted her to stop but I said to carry on. There was nothing more specific other than the message that all my spirit family are there for me to talk to at any time and to just feel the love.

Chapter 14

Finally I had a buyer for the house. Two years of serious struggling and constantly turning the heating off when the lodgers were out even in a freezing winter, were soon to be over. I am pretty sure that 100% of the people who came to my house during this period said that it was warmer outside than in! Obviously the heating was on when the children were there and the lodgers but I had been lucky to find Monday to Friday lodgers so matter how cold it was, the heating was always off when I was alone. The six years living in the flat in Hall Green growing up had prepared me for this as we had no central heating there, but now I was older, I was cold. A lot of the time.

As soon as I realised that the house sale was going through, my thoughts turned to living by the sea. It had been a dream of mine for so many years and the family holidays as a child to Devon and Cornwall had encouraged that dream. Family holidays we had also enjoyed in recent years in Devon, increased my desire for a life away from the rat race of city and town living. Although we hard largely lived in the countryside, the daily drips to Birmingham for work and school were soul destroying.

One holiday in St Mawes staying at the beautiful Tresanton Hotel was superb. We had a fantastic family suite above the main hotel looking out to sea.

I told Peter that it would be my absolute dream to live here and see this view every day. "Don't be so ridiculous," he exclaimed, "you're a city girl through and through. You'd last five minutes in a place like this." That was in the year 2000.

I decided to visit Cornwall first and so started an internet search looking for a property to renovate whilst living in it. My friends Roger and Gill whose son Samuel was buried in the churchyard near to Henry had moved to Cornwall a few years previously and on the odd occasions I saw them, said they knew it would be perfect for me.

I didn't find anything in particular that really told my instinct to go for in Cornwall although I saw some beautiful places. Plenty of the villages have suffered badly in the recession and no longer have a store, public house or school.

Earlier on in the year, two old school friends, Carol and Martin and I had organized a school reunion for our secondary school to see if we could meet up thirty years after we had left. We each worked on a list to contact people via Friends Reunited, Facebook, Linkedin etc. and Google searches. I must give him the credit he deserves here and Martin worked the hardest! Stirling effort!

I did a google search on Chris who was my first proper boyfriend when I was fourteen. In those days you would say that you were going out with someone even if you didn't go anywhere! I still had a fondness for him, here we go again with that word, even though I hadn't seen him for many many years since we had left college.

This search linked to a site advertising a home available for a holiday let in Devon. There was an instant messaging page where you e mail the owner through the site. Therefore my e mail read, "Hi firstly, sorry if I have the wrong person, but it's Julie here, your old friend from school. There is a school reunion happening soon and we would like you to come. Apologies again, if this is the wrong person."

The following day, I received a lovely warm reply, saying that yes it was the right person and what a wonderful surprise to hear from me after all these years!

Unfortunately Chris couldn't make the reunion but we stayed in touch. Therefore, when I told him of my plans to move south, he said that I must visit so that we could catch up. He urged that I should choose Devon over Cornwall as the latter was so bleak in the winter. In fact my friend Gill confirmed that although she loved living in Cornwall, Devon was much prettier.

I arranged to meet Chris at the Cider Press Centre in Dartington at a cafe. As I sat there waiting for him to arrive, the enormity of what I was doing engulfed me. But my instinct was marching on faster and I was running to keep up with it. You need a rest, my mind body and soul was ordering this and it was a well deserved one at that.

I ordered a pot of tea and sat outside the cafe. When I saw Chris running down the path from the car park, my heart skipped a beat! He was still so handsome, and he had retained his boyish good looks even though he had lost some hair. I struggled to contain myself.

"I can't believe this is happening can you?" started Chris and we hugged and politely kissed on each other's cheek.

We worked out that it had been twenty eight years since we had last seen each other. There was a lot to catch up on. But the talk flowed easily. Friends from long ago chatting as if all of those years hadn't happened. We caught up on the detail of our lives, such as children, marriage and work.

Chris explained that as well as running his business teaching outdoor pursuits to children, he was also a professional storyteller and had a secret to tell me which he hoped I wouldn't be annoyed about.

I was stunned that he thought I should be annoyed about anything and clearly had no idea what he was talking about but said that no whatever it was, he should tell me and I wouldn't be cross.

"Well," he started, "when we were fourteen, and I took you to the cinema to see a film I didn't want to watch, The China Syndrome, do you remember what happened next?"

I recounted how I remembered the times we had spent in each other's homes and the amount of kissing we had enjoyed including on that Saturday in the cinema but I wasn't sure what Chris meant by what happened next.

He then reminded me that although we had endured a tediously boring film not destined for two fourteen year olds, how he taken almost the length of the film to put his arm around me and kiss me. Yes I remembered this very clearly, but what was his point?

"Well then I made the fatal mistake of moving my right hand to your right breast and you sharply pulled my hand away. On the Monday morning at school you very succinctly announced that in the light of my behaviour on Saturday afternoon, that you no longer wished to go out with me. I was crushed, simply crushed. Heartbroken. Here and now I have to tell you that the first kiss we had was the best kiss of my life. So, therefore, as part of my work dealing with adolescents, I tell young boys in particular of my story with you. I can assure you I have told this story many times in order to warn them of being too familiar too soon as I had and making a catastrophic mistake."

I now could have been knocked down by a feather. "I am so

sorry Chris, I had no idea that I had hurt you like that. I didn't even remember the cause of us not seeing each other any more and yet it had stayed in his memory so vividly, that he chose to recount if often. I couldn't suppress a feeling that if he wanted to touch my right or even left breast now, then he was more than welcome. But I didn't tell him.

He then announced that although he didn't know what was on the table for dinner that evening at his house, I was welcome to join them. As this was now almost six o'clock, I said that it was best for me to get going as I had the two hundred miles to drive home.

But Chris insisted and I followed him in my car. He was going through a divorce from the mother of his children he had explained, and he had an Australian girlfriend.

The girlfriend didn't seem too impressed at my presence but she had cooked a lovely meal and we sat and chatted with ease about old school friends and what we had been doing with our lives.

Chris gave me a few pointers on the area regarding property as he had lived here for twelve years and he urged me again to consider Devon over Cornwall due to the latter being so quiet and bleak in the winter. He felt that I would cope better moving from a large town to this area rather than somewhere more remote. Even though most of my married life had been spent living in the countryside, it was only ten minutes drive from a large town and thirty minutes from our second city.

That evening as I left, I apologised to Chris once more for the unceremonious and pompous way in which I had dumped him all those years ago and drove back up the M5 motorway. Mandy Honey had mentioned Chris to me as a significant friend in the future.

The journey home was full now of opportunities of where I would live. I told everyone of my plans and gave myself the 'get out' clause of saying that this would be a six to twelve month project in case I didn't like it. After two years of really struggling to pay the bills, I could now get rid of my debts and buy a property whilst more importantly drastically reducing my stress levels.

When I informed Richard who was handling my house sale in Solihull of my intentions, he thought it was a great, bold decision and being a fan of and frequent visitor to Devon himself, was envious. He pondered whether I would be like another client of his, Birmingham born and bred, a proper Brummie in his words, who had relocated to St Mawes a few years previously. This client had surprisingly settled into his new life with such ease, that he now felt in a state of panic driving up the M5 to visit relatives, so much so that when he reached Exeter, he considered turning round and driving back.

This is a feeling I know well. Naturally my visits to see my children, father and friends are frequent and I love seeing them, but I do get in a panic now driving in the traffic. The traffic here is getting stuck behind a tractor for five minutes. It is a complete culture shock going back to the Midlands. In fact on my last visit to Birmingham, going up the escalators in the Bull Ring gave me such an attack of vertigo, I had to get off and go down in the lift. Everywhere is so busy, but here I can have a little holiday everyday if I so choose. The air is cleaner, and the stress, despite this transient marriage I am still in, is less. The people here enjoy a much slower pace of life. True Devonians rarely leave the area and regularly stay living where they were born. It is not a joke to say that they refer to everywhere north of Exeter, as 'the north'. They do. All of them, with the exception of the odd one or two talking of 'somewhere up country'. It is like living in a different world on a different planet here and I like it. All those years of racing around at a hundred miles an hour, started to seem like a lifetime away.

In December 2011, when I moved to Ipplepen, a place I've nick named the 'village of the damned' as although there are some lovely people there, there are some decidedly odd ones too, my cousin John came to visit me. He declared that he had never seen me look more calm and at peace. The stress of the last few years had been washed away from my face.

"You want to be careful just landing here on your own. There will be blokes in this village after you, you're a good catch." I laughed and said that I needed a rest, and the last thing I was looking for was a bloke and I certainly wasn't going to get married again.

I suppose to the villagers it seemed odd that I had indeed landed here on my own from that place they all call 'the north.' But people were very friendly and some came and knocked on my door to introduce themselves. I had been invited to two parties in the first month.

I met Mark shortly after moving there and a year later we got married. Mark used to live in Plymouth and he was very keen on history especially Greek history. The first time he took me out for lunch was to the Royal William yard in Plymouth.

Invading my new found calm, Peter and Chris then complained about me to the Ombudsman regarding the pension plan who decided that the plan be closed down due to the timing involved. It was also stated that whilst Peter and Chris could not dismiss the handwriting report (which stated that I had not signed the documents but the evidence pointed to Peter) I had commissioned, as they had done, I should have known that I was a trustee. So they got away with it and the

£11,000 which turned into £50,000 turned into a lot more in my name but I didn't get to the bottom of the true story. The Vicar once said to me that the truth always comes out in the end. Even if takes fifty years.

Chapter 15

The last year has been one I have endured through gritted teeth. When my second husband, during an argument about him asking me for investment, for his failing business which had raged on all day, punched me directly in the face, I could not feel any more desperate seeing my dreadfully swollen face in the mirror just hours later. Four hours of x rays in the hospital revealed miraculously, no broken bones. I am surprised I didn't lose my teeth, such was the force of the blow.

I do not deserve this I thought, there are no second chances when someone makes you look like you have been in a car accident. But I had made a grave error of judgment in my desire to settle down and have the quiet peaceful life I had always yearned.

When the word mania is used describing someone's reaction to abruptly ceasing with their medication, it is like watching an out of control train hurtling along. Mark's demons are his and his alone to fix. It can't be so difficult to take a tablet each day and go to counselling once a week. I say this without much sympathy, due to being on the receiving end of his rages so many times.

The children would like me to move closer and I have considered all options, so that maybe when this house is sold I can buy a small flat here and a home nearer to them. If only I could take the sea up there, so then I would have everything all in one place.

A few weeks ago, I was in the village post office and joined in a conversation that the postmaster, who is also the local coastguard, (that's what it's like round here), was having with a fellow customer. They were discussing all the main newspapers, and in particular the online versions.

When the other customer had left, the postmaster informed me that the other customer was a freelance journalist and had a column in The Times. He explained that he had queried some of the journalist's stories where he had written about things which had supposedly happened in the village.

"I think he makes some of it up!" the postmaster declared.

I started writing this book six years ago and have picked it up and dropped it many times during those years. Following that conversation in the post office firmly had my mind made up that I should get on and finish what I had started. My story isn't made up. It is all true.

I am not happy with the way parts of my life have turned out but delighted that my remaining four children and now beautiful delightful granddaughter are all healthy and happy. That will be my legacy. My children and theirs'.

I hope I have many more years to live. Life is different for me now as I can never be truly happy, and I miss my astral travelling times. Dreams are an escape instead.

Wish me luck on the rest of my soul's journey. I wish you love, luck, fulfilment and joy on yours'...

August 2014